Here's what people are saying about *Halftime*:

This is a book that should be read by people in both halves of their lives. It is a book that I would hope my children would read as they start their professional careers, using it as a guide and road map to figure out their lives for themselves. It is a book that should be read and reread by those of us in or reaching the second half. It is a book that challenges the reader to action, and in taking that action, to greater service to themselves, their families, their communities, and their Maker.

Peter H. Coors, CEO, Coors Brewing Company

This inspiring book comes out of the mind and heart of a truly remarkable individual and addresses an enormous need in our society — how to find meaning and fulfillment in the second half of our lives. In short, how to move from success to significance!

Stephen R. Covey, Covey Leadership Center

Bob Buford is one of those rare individuals who has made the transition from focusing on success to focusing on significance. This book will show you how to make the rest of your life the best of your life. I want every man in my congregation to read this inspiring story!

Rick Warren, pastor, Saddleback Community Church

Bob's approach really hits squarely at the feelings and the emotions in a way that possibly only a fellow Christian businessman, like Bob, can do.

Steven S. Reinemund, chairman and CEO, Pepsico, Inc.

According to Bob Buford, the first half of life is a quest for success; the second is a quest for significance. Bob should know; he has achieved the first and is showing us the latter. You'll find this book to be unique, inspiring, and practical. Read it and finish strong!

Max Lucado, *New York Times* Bestselling Author
of *When God Whispers Your Name*

I am someone who has benefited immeasurably from the second half of Bob Buford's life. He is one of the most effective kingdom catalysts I know.

Bill Hybels, senior pastor,
Willow Creek Community Church

Bob's book makes us listen to those gnawing doubts we have about our approach to work and life; and then, in an easily read style, gives us a way to analyze our options for doing better and for finding the courage to act.

Dennis Bakke, CEO emeritus, The AES Corporation

This book is for successful people who want more fulfillment in their lives and realize it won't come from the next victory, the next sale, the next conquest, or significant increase in their bottom line. Let Bob Buford be your guide to make sure your best years are ahead of you.

Ken Blanchard, coauthor of *The One-Minute Manager*

Mr. Buford writes for the private chambers of the heart. For my part, just crossing forty, *Halftime* is received like a cup of cold water for a restless man, breathless at midrace but gathered for the final run.

David G. Bradley, chairman, Atlantic Media Company

Bob Buford's *Halftime* is not only a powerful message; it's a spur to personal action. It's sincere and practical. It's moving and compelling.... I thank Bob for sharing his life story and his philosophy for a better tomorrow.

Michael J. Kami, Consultancy in Strategic Management

For all who want to connect (or reconnect) passion with purpose, success with significance, and crowds with community, Bob Buford's words and life offer a graceful call to learn how to live what we believe. In the deepest and original sense, his is a "re-formed" life, a life that has been wonderfully shaped by his primary loyalty.

Don Flow, president, Flow Motors, Inc.

This book reveals the heart of a man who uses his time and talent for God and the care of people throughout the world. Down through the centuries God has especially blessed those men and women who have a good heart, and Bob is one of those. The message of this book will make a valuable contribution.

Douglas E. Coe, who through his work has developed many close relationships with members of Congress, Washington, D.C.

This is the book I am giving to my children.

Max DePree, chairman, Herman Miller, Inc.; author of *Leadership Jazz* and *Leadership Is an Art*

For many years I've encouraged Christians to dream great dreams, plan great plans, pray great prayers, and obey God's great commands. Drawing on his business acumen and commitment to Jesus Christ, Bob Buford helps you do just that. He incites you to multiply all that God has given you to live a truly significant life.

Luis Palau, Luis Palau Evangelistic Association

Halftime is a fascinating story of spectacular success in business moving to spectacular significance in serving others. It holds not only Bob Buford's philosophy, but quotations from many wonderfully diverse philosophers on their spiritual journeys. It is a book for first- and second-halfers and for all those who appreciate a warmly personal odyssey.

Frances Hesselbein, president and CEO,
The Drucker Foundation

There are many rich young rulers who will be in heaven because of Bob Buford's life. Now he has created a brilliant work on how to stop counting the years and start making the years count. I know this will make my second half more meaningful.

Stephen Arterburn, founder and chairman, New Life Ministries

Bob's book challenges us to stop and think about the directions and priorities of our lives. Having struggled through the transitions in a life fully examined and engaged, his insights and advice ring true and deep. His kind of coaching, derived from having played the game with skill and grace, is filled with wisdom that equips us with principles and strategies that enrich our lives.

J. Williams, chairman, Trammell Crow Company

Bob Buford knows that in life, as in sports, it is important to finish well. What good are great stats in the first half if you come up short at the end? In a way success-minded Americans can understand, Bob gives a locker room pep talk on discovering life's basics. If you wonder if you have the right game plan for your life, call a time-out and read this book.

Stephen A. Hayner, PhD, associate professor
of Evangelism and Church Growth,
Columbia Theological Seminary

UPDATED AND EXPANDED

HALF
Moving from Success to Significance®
TIME®

BOB BUFORD

www.Halftime.org

ZONDERVAN®

We want to hear from you. Please send your comments about this book to us in care of zreview@zondervan.com. Thank you.

ZONDERVAN

Halftime®
Copyright © 1994, 2008 by The Leadership Network, Inc.

This title is also available in a Zondervan audio edition.
Visit www.zondervan.fm.

Requests for information should be addressed to:

Zondervan, *Grand Rapids, Michigan* 49530

Library of Congress Cataloging-in-Publication Data

Buford, Bob.
    Halftime : changing your game plan from success to significance / Bob Buford. —
Updated and expanded ed.
       p.   cm.
    Includes bibliographical references and index.
    ISBN 978-0-310-28424-6 (hardcover, jacketed)
      1. Middle-aged persons — Religious life. 2. Middle-aged persons — Psychology.
    3. Self-realization — Religious aspects — Christianity. I. Title.
    BV4579.5.B84   2008
    248.8'42 — dc22   2008024288

"Questions for Reflection and Discussion" prepared by Lyn Cryderman
Interior design: Beth Shagene

Printed in the United States of America

*To the two most important
people in my life:
Linda,
the woman who has shaped my heart,
and
the late Peter Drucker,
the man who formed my mind.*

Contents

PART 3
THE SECOND HALF

Preface

Fifteen years ago I began recording my thoughts about something that happened in my life. Instead of facing a crisis as I approached middle age, I discovered that a new and better life lay before me. I called the process of discovery "halftime," and the eventual outcome of this process led to my "second half." The metaphor fit because, after a successful first half, I needed a break to make some changes in how I played the second. I had plenty of success over the preceding twenty years, and I wasn't burned out or frustrated, but I felt something was missing and I needed to change my game plan. In retrospect I can see that I must have been divinely protected from chasing down the usual trails people take to find what was missing.

I took what I had written to a publisher who decided to turn it into a book for which he had modest expectations. Since then, it is safe to say a movement has evolved around *Halftime*. More than 500,000 people have read this book, the majority of them using it as a catalyst to discover their own second half. The organization I founded, Leadership Network, responded to the thousands of letters I received by creating the Halftime Group, which provides resources and coaching to personally guide others through the journey from success to significance. People continue to buy the book in significant numbers, and the Halftime Group is busier than ever. Apparently the still, small voice that spoke to me about changing my game plan more than twenty years ago sounds familiar to people today, so familiar that my publisher asked me to revise and update the book.

In many ways, I have changed nothing. My message is the same today as it was in 1994: if you are approaching middle age — which can be anywhere from your late thirties well into your fifties — the very best years of your life lie ahead of you. Whatever success you are having will never completely fulfill you. A life of significance — of really mattering — is yours for the taking, and the process I describe in this book will work for you.

When I first wrote the book, however, few people owned cell phones and fewer still had access to the Internet. People whose stories I've told have passed on to a better place, and better resources exist to help you on your way. So I carved out some time at my farm in Tyler, Texas, to reread the book with one question in mind: if I were to start over today, what would I change? As it turned out, not much, but enough to make this book a better resource for your journey. New, updated stories of people who have discovered their second-half mission. A brand-new chapter addressing the question, "How can I experience halftime if I can't quit my job?" A revised set of questions for discussion at the end of the book. And coaching infused with the wisdom of those who read the book and learned something new as they began their second-half adventure.

Perhaps the best feature of the original edition was the wonderful foreword my friend and mentor Peter Drucker wrote. Sadly, Peter passed away on November 11, 2005. His introductory words still ring true, so I have kept his foreword. But another good friend of mine and Peter's, bestselling author Jim Collins, has written another foreword that is every bit as good as Peter's — a bonus for me as well as you.

Enjoy.

Foreword

Bob Buford has a peculiar genius for inspiring people to embrace discomfort. I first met Bob in 1996 when he asked me to teach pastors from large evangelical churches. I knew nothing about megachurches, and I wondered if I could possibly contribute to their thinking. "All the more reason to do it!" responded Buford. "It will force you to learn something new that you can contribute to others. You have no idea what you will learn when you engage these church leaders — and that will make you more useful."

Bob turned out to be right about the learning adventure. Partway through the megachurch session, while I was encouraging pastors to create churches built to last, a hand shot up in the back.

"Jim, now why is this important?" queried a pastor from South Carolina.

"Because if you don't think ahead about succession — if your church depends just on you and your charismatic personality — it will likely decline or fall after you leave." I then shared the story of a once-great company whose aging founder defined succession planning as merely prefacing a statement every month or so with "If I happen to be unavailable ..."

The pastor looked at me almost with pity, as if I'd somehow missed first grade, then said in a slow, deliberate drawl, "Now, Mr. Collins, I think you're, ah, missing a fundamental point here," pausing for effect. "See, our founder" — another pause — "well, he's *never* unavailable."

The room erupted into laughter, and I noticed Buford nodding at me, as if to say, "See, I told you that you'd be pushed by this and you'd be better for it." I went home and rethought the built-to-last ideas in the context of religious leadership, and thus began a lasting friendship that has been a continual source of renewal for me.

Buford kept pushing and challenging. During one of our long conversations, I asked Buford (who happens to be the best emissary for Christianity I've yet to meet), "How did Christianity transform itself from a handful of fanatics wandering around a remote backwater of the Roman Empire into the official religion of the most powerful empire in the world three hundred years later? To use an analogy, it would be like two dozen people starting a new religion thirty miles from Baghdad today and turning it into the official religion of the United States a century or two down the road — and doing it without any mass communication. How did this happen?" Buford responded by asking knowledgeable Christian historians, collecting their answers, and sending me a banker's box of data and information to read and digest — another challenge, another opportunity for learning and renewal, another Bob Buford jolt.

There is a delicious irony in Bob's asking me to pen this foreword: I'm right smack in the middle of halftime, as I'm turning fifty. Buford slyly got me to engage with his work at the very moment when it will do me the most good. I do not have the answers, but Buford has given me — and all those who read his book — the right question: Why capitulate to irrelevance after we've spent decades accumulating empirical wisdom?

In the first half of the twentieth century, people largely viewed work as a necessary evil, a way to provide security and comfort. Then, in the 1960s, people began to demand more from their careers — they wanted meaning and a sense of purpose. And now Bob Buford comes along with the next challenge: to think beyond the narrow bounds of a satisfying and successful career to a meaningful and useful entire life. Here in *Halftime*, he asserts that the old model of arduous career followed by relaxing retirement should be jettisoned, replaced by the idea that the second half can — and should — be *more* creative, *more* impactful, *more* meaningful, *more* adventurous, and filled with *more* learning and contribution than the first half. A successful first fifty years should be viewed as nothing more than a good start.

Most who read Buford's work have already attained success and find it wanting. And when we reach halftime, when we know we have fewer days ahead than behind — when our mentors and teachers and moms and dads begin to die — the idea of just "more success" does not answer the question, "What's the point?" Have you answered the question, "What's the one thing — not two things, not three, not four, but the *one big thing* — in the box?" Have you written your own epitaph? Have you articulated a strategy for multiplying your contribution by 100X? Have you answered, "How much is enough?" Have you done "seismic testing" to discover where you can best be of service? Have you organized your time around two essential elements of a complete life: self-realization and community? If you're ready for these questions, you're ready for *Halftime*.

In puzzling over Buford's questions, I've come to see two distinct approaches to self-renewal — and I encourage you to consider both as you read this book. The first lies in the late John Gardner's idea of repotting ourselves into entirely new activities as we move from success to significance, changing our activities from career to contribution. Gardner, former secretary of health, education, and welfare (and author of the classic *Self-Renewal*), once told me that he planned to learn and grow as much between ages seventy and eighty-eight as between zero and eighteen. When challenged, Gardner said that he knew a little bit more about learning at seventy than when he was zero. Gardner pushed people to think about "repotting" themselves every ten to fifteen years, throwing themselves into challenges that extract hidden strengths. Buford picks up where Gardner left off, challenging us to see that some of our most significant and meaningful contributions should come in the second half, defying the view that creativity wanes with age. By repotting, you can recreate the sense of excitement and imagination experienced in your teens or twenties — again and again and again. Repotting also has the wonderful side benefit of slowing down time. Think about how vivid your experience was the first few weeks of moving to a new school, new city, new company, or new country — the very newness heightened your senses and deepened your memories — compared with how you experienced the fiftieth or one hundredth week, when life had become routine.

The second path to self-renewal lies in seeing your primary activity — the same activity you've pursued for your first half — as the primary means to renewal. For some, the best choice lies on the second path, choosing to renew *within* a chosen genre or field, much as an artist grows within his or her craft. Beethoven didn't reach halftime and then give up music to renew; he stayed focused and created some of his most radical, path-breaking music. Would Beethoven been of more use giving up music to find significance? Like Beethoven, Peter Drucker took the second path, and it is entirely fitting that Drucker wrote the first foreword to this book.

Drucker's books fill three bookshelves at Claremont Graduate University; as a Claremont friend of mine pointed out, "Notice that his writings *before* age sixty-five sit on one shelf and his writings *after* sixty-five require two shelves." When I asked Peter Drucker, then age eighty-six, which of his twenty-six books he was proudest of, he responded, "The next one." For some, being a CEO (or a writer or a church leader or a professor) is their art, and if this describes you, the question becomes, if you've only written four symphonies by halftime, what will be symphonies 5, 6, 7, 8, and 9 — and how can you make your ninth symphony the most extraordinary of all?

So, be forewarned before you become acquainted with Bob Buford through the pages that follow. Do not read this book if you want your life to be easy and comfortable. Do not read this book if you want to coast to the finish line. Do not read this book if you want mainly to take rather than give. But if you have a deep desire to be of use, to learn and to grow right up until the day you die, you'll find *Halftime* an invigorating challenge.

The question of renewal stays with us for our entire lives. Some answer the question with tremendous grace and creativity, becoming "seventy years young"; others, sadly, begin to age early, reaching half-seventy at "thirty-five years old." And while Buford has employed the halftime analogy with tremendous effect, there remains one huge difference between a sport and life: in football (or in a marathon or on a mountain climb) you know exactly when you have crossed the halfway mark. In life you might think you have reached halftime but in fact be at mile twenty-five of the twenty-six-mile marathon, or in the last two minutes of the fourth quarter, or perhaps — if fortunate — still only a third of the way up the mountain. We only get one life, and the urgency of getting on with what we are meant to do increases every day. The clock is ticking.

JIM COLLINS
Boulder, Colorado
November 2007

Foreword to First Edition

This is a most unusual, indeed a unique, book — at least I do not know of any book that is even remotely similar.

It is immediately accessible as the autobiography of an unusual man and can be read as such with great pleasure. It is the story of obscure beginnings, the story of a boy who, barely eleven, after his father's early death, had to take on the burden of being the "man of the family"; a story of great hardships, of vision and determination, of sorrow and success.

While this in itself is interesting, what is unusual is that Bob Buford is one of the very few people I know who, still barely in his teens, thought through what his strengths were. This is something that, as a rule, only a few artists do. Even more incredible is that, when he realized that what the Lord had made him capable of doing well was very different from what he really *wanted* to do, he had the intellectual honesty and courage to say to himself, "It is my duty and mission to put to work what I am good at, rather than to do what I would love to do." To this, of course, Bob owes his success as entrepreneur and businessman.

But — and this, in my experience, is truly unprecedented — Bob never forgot his original vision and never surrendered his original values to success. He refused to write off his youthful ambition as a child's dream. He kept his nose to the grindstone and yet never lost sight of the hills. And when, after thirty years of unremitting toil, he had reached the point where he could spare some time and some money, he then thought through again how to accomplish what he had wanted to do thirty years earlier, but to do so by putting his strengths, his experience, and his knowledge to work.

At this same point, many people retire. But Bob realized that he liked, indeed loved, his work and was very good at it. He knew that he should keep on doing what he was doing. But he also determined that the time had come for him to develop a parallel career in which his strengths, his knowledge, his experience — and his money — would serve his deep personal commitment to advance the kingdom of God on earth; that is, to serve Christianity in his native land.

This is unusual enough. But at the same time, this book is far more than an autobiography. Without preaching, without trying to be "scholarly," without statistics and academic jargon, this book tackles the fundamental *social* challenge of a developed and affluent society such as ours has become.

Not so long ago, when I was born a few years before World War I, few people lived beyond what we now consider early middle age. As late as 1929, average life expectancy in the United States was not even fifty years — and half a century earlier it had been around thirty-five. But today the great majority of Americans — and of people in developed countries altogether — can expect to live twice as long as people could expect to live at the time of our great-grandparents.

Equally important, for the first time in history, a very large number of people can expect to be "successes" — something that, in the past, was practically unknown. Success does not necessarily mean a substantial fortune or even great worldly success. But it does mean attaining something that those in earlier times simply did not know: achievement, perhaps as a professor in a college, as a physician or lawyer, as a middle manager or professional in an organization, or as a hospital administrator — all jobs which, at the beginning of the century, either did not exist at all or were so few in numbers as to be socially insignificant.

Back then, work was a living, not a life. The worker in the steel plant, the farmer on the traditional family farm, the worker on the assembly line, the salesperson in the small mom-and-pop shop — all people in traditional employments — were perfectly ready to retire after thirty years, if only they could afford it. They did not miss their work, since it was never anything but a means to get their next meal on the table or to pay for the children's shoes.

Today a growing number of people expect to find what Bob Buford found: that they enjoy their work, that they become better as they become older, that they are not ready to retire even though they may have the means to do so. A large and growing number of people — I call them "knowledge workers" — not only do much better financially than anybody in history has ever done, they do infinitely better in terms of personal fulfillment. And yet when they reach their midforties, the work they know and love is no longer challenging. They need new stimulus.

When I first became aware of this some twenty or thirty years ago, I thought that there would be an enormous number of "second career" people who would move from being, for instance, divisional controller in a big company to doing similar work in a nonprofit institution. I was wrong — Bob Buford taught me better. The great majority of these people do not want to leave what they are doing and what they are good at. But they do feel the need to add what Bob calls "the other half of their lives," what I would call "a parallel career." They want to find the sphere in which they can serve their values by putting to work what they're good at, using the strengths, knowledge, and experience they've already gained.

These are new challenges, unprecedented ones, as I said before. And this book is the first one, to my knowledge, that masterfully presents them and shows how to address them. This is pioneering of a high order. This is social analysis of a high order.

And it is also a self-help book of the highest order. Whatever one's values and commitments — and they need not be at all those of Bob Buford — this book should be the catalyst for all those who are the beneficiaries of the two great social developments of this century: the extension of life span (especially of working life span), and the fact that it is now possible to be a "success" and to make a life out of one's living.

This is an important *political* book as well. We increasingly realize that modern government is not capable of taking care of community and social problems. Nor is the free market. There is a growing awareness of the need for a new sector — whether you call it "nonprofit," "third sector," "independent sector," or (my own preference) "social sector." In this sector, citizenship as a working "volunteer" once again becomes a reality rather than a ritual consisting of voting once in a while and paying taxes. Bob's book indicates the solution to the major political challenge of a developed society: that middle-aged success can help restore the body politic to function, to effectiveness, and to a reaffirmation of the basic values of both democracy and community.

This is also a *religious* book that goes to the heart of one of America's major challenges: the role of religion and Christianity in American society and in the life of America's people. Everybody knows that most of the mainstream churches in America have been steadily losing members in the last thirty or forty years. But what is amazing is not that the churches have lost members, but that they have lost so few! For the church membership of yesterday — and yesterday means only fifty or sixty years ago — was in a good many cases the result of social compulsion rather than free choice.

When I first came to this country in the '30s as an American correspondent for a group of British papers, church attendance was mandatory. The application for a mortgage that we filled out within a few weeks of our moving to this country — and in an affluent and hardly "religious" New York City suburb to boot — asked for two references, one of whom had to be the pastor of the church you attended. If you had no such reference, you could not get a mortgage. Even twenty-five years later, in the early '50s, in small town and rural America, somebody who did not go to church did not get a bank loan or a decent job.

This social pressure has now disappeared. But although we may have expected, as a result, a catastrophic decline in church membership, the decline has been modest by any standard — let alone by comparison with Europe — and it is being counteracted by the growth of the new, large "pastoral churches" that are growing in membership two or three times faster than the conventional churches are losing members. America, in other words, is still very much a Christian country, provided the churches learn how to serve today's constituencies: people who do not go to church because they are virtually forced to do so, but who go to church because they prefer it to everything else.

To have seen this early was one of Bob's great insights. His Leadership Network worked as a catalyst to make the large, pastoral churches work effectively, to identify their main problems, to make them capable of perpetuating themselves (as no earlier pastoral church has ever been able to do), and to focus them on their mission as apostles, witnesses, and central community services. And now he is extending this work to many churches, including midsized ones, not as a preacher but as an entrepreneur who converts latent energies into performance.

Finally, this book can — and should — be read as a story of growth from knowledge into wisdom, of intellectual and spiritual education. Such stories are rare indeed — and far more exciting, important, and instructive than swashbuckling adventure or "romantic" derring-do. These are the stories needed by those who have reached the middle of their life span, the ones who have become successful in the sense that they have achieved — just as the very young need the stories of heroic exploits and of romantic love.

This is, to conclude, a book that should and will be read on many levels. It is a book that will speak differently to different people. But it is a book that will have meaning and message for all those who open its pages.

PETER F. DRUCKER
September 1, 1994

Opening the Heart's Holiest Chamber

Then he told them many things in parables, saying: "A farmer went out to sow his seed. As he was scattering the seed, some fell along the path, and the birds came and ate it up. Some fell on rocky places, where it did not have much soil. It sprang up quickly, because the soil was shallow. But when the sun came up, the plants were scorched, and they withered because they had no root. Other seed fell among thorns, which grew up and choked the plants. Still other seed fell on good soil, where it produced a crop—a hundred, sixty or thirty times what was sown. Whoever has ears, let them hear."

Matthew 13:3–9

None of us knows when we will die. But any one of us, if we wish, may select our own epitaph. I have chosen mine. It is, I should confess, a somewhat haunting thing to think about your gravestone while you are vitally alive. Yet there it is, a vivid image in my mind and heart, standing as both a glorious inspiration and an epic challenge to me:

100X

It means "100 times." I have taken it for myself from the parable of the sower in Matthew 13. I'm an entrepreneur, and I want to be remembered as the seed that was planted in good soil and multiplied a hundredfold. It is how I wish to live. It is how I attempt to express my passions and my core commitments. It is how I envision my own legacy. I want to be a symbol of higher yield, in life and in death.

Augustine said that asking yourself the question of your own legacy — *What do I wish to be remembered for?* — is the beginning of adulthood. That is what I have done by writing my own epitaph. After all, an epitaph should be something more than a wispy, wishful, self-selected motto. If it's honest, it says something about who you are at the essence of your personality and your soul.

The stuff that stirs within the heart's holiest chamber is, I believe, a gift given to us all by our Creator. It's one way of expressing a conviction that human beings are more than animals or machines. It's a confession that we are spiritual beings with a purpose — and a destiny. It's a divine reminder that we are miraculously and wonderfully made in the image of God.

You may call my 100X epitaph wishful thinking, and surely that is part of what it is. But when you select an epitaph as an expression of gratitude for your singular talent — and as a goal to which you are committed until you rest, at last, beneath the gravestone — you identify yourself as someone with a purpose and a passion that has been encoded in you for life.

Jesus taught primarily by telling stories or parables, and the parable of the sower gets to the center of my dreams and to the kernel of my experiences. It is the driving force behind this book. My passion is to multiply all that God has given me and, in the process, give it back. And I would like to incite you to do the same. I do not want you to be the seed that fell along the path or was scattered in rocky places or was choked by weeds. Such seed held the potential to become fruitful, but circumstances prevented it.

My own circumstances provided a moist and fertile soil in which I could grow. It was a fortunate environment, and that has been a critical factor in my story. My own tale is not that of the self-made man, nor is it a rags-to-riches account or a Horatio Alger fantasy. I was given far more opportunity for growth, personal development, and financial rewards than most Americans.

On the one hand, you might say that I have been lucky, for indeed I have been given much with which to work. But if you believe, as I do, that "to whom much is given, much is also required," you will begin to see how daunting my epitaph is.

What about your epitaph? What have you been given, and what will you do with it the rest of your life?

Recently, I have begun looking at my own life through the metaphor of a football game (actually, any sport that divides its action into two halves will do). Up until my thirty-fifth year, I was in the first half. Then circumstances intervened that sent me into halftime. Now I am playing the second half, and it's turning into a great game. Along the way, I have come to the conclusion that the second half of our lives should be the best half — that it can be, in fact, a personal renaissance.

During the first half of your life, if you are like me, you probably did not have time to think about how you would spend the rest of your life. You probably rushed through college, fell in love, married, embarked on a career, climbed upward, and acquired a few things to help make the journey comfortable.

You played a hard-fought first half. You even may have been winning. But sooner or later you begin to wonder if this really is as good as it gets. Somehow, keeping score does not offer the thrill it once did.

You may have taken some vicious hits. A good share of men and women never make it to halftime without pain. Serious pain. Divorce. Too much alcohol. Not enough time for your kids. Guilt. Loneliness. Like many good players, you started the half with good intentions but got blindsided along the way.

Even if your pain was slight, you are smart enough to see that you cannot play the second half as you did the first. For one thing, you do not have the energy you once had. Fresh out of college, you had no problem with working fourteen-hour days and working extra hours on your days off. It was part of your first-half game plan, something almost inevitable if you hoped to succeed. But now you yearn for something more than success.

Then there is the reality of the game itself: The clock is running. What once looked like an eternity ahead of you is now within reach. And while you do not fear the end of the game, you do want to make sure that you finish well, that you leave something behind that no one can take away from you. If the first half was a quest for success, the second half is a journey to significance.

The game is won or lost in the second half, not the first. It's possible to make some mistakes in the first half and still have time to recover, but it's harder to do that in the second half. In the second half, you should, at long last, know what you have to work with. And you know the playing field — the world you live in. You have experienced enough victory to know how hard the game is most of the time yet how easy it seems when the conditions are just right. You have experienced enough pain and disappointment to know that while losing a few rounds is certainly no fun, loss is survivable and sometimes uncovers the best that is in you.

Some people never get to the second half; a good many don't even know it exists. The prevailing view in our culture is that as you close out your fortieth year or so, you enter a period of aging and decline. To pair age with *growth* seems to be a contradiction in terms. This is a myth I refuse to believe, and I want to help you shatter it as well.

I do not know where you are in the game. If you are in your twenties, you have probably just received the opening kickoff and have an exciting half ahead of you. Much of what I write will seem far-off to you, but do not put this book where you won't be able to find it later, for the first half races by faster than you think.

It's likely that you are nearing the end of the half. You are in your midthirties to early forties and something has been telling you that you cannot keep playing as you have been. This book will speak most clearly to you.

Or you may even be in the second half but have never really thought of it that way. Like a good lineman, you just kept charging ahead. This book may lead you to call time-out, head for the sidelines, and take stock, for it is never too late to change your game plan.

Regardless of where you are, I invite you, in the following pages, to discredit the view that the second half of your life will never measure up to the first. Instead of giving up and settling for life on its own terms, you are ready for new horizons, new challenges. You are ready to move from success to significance — to write your own epitaph — daring to believe that what you ultimately leave behind will be more important than anything you could have achieved in the first half of your life.

PART 1

THE FIRST HALF

*The real test of a man is not when he plays
the role that he wants for himself,
but when he plays the role destiny has for him.*
Vaclav Havel

CHAPTER 1

Listening to the Gentle Whisper

Then a great and powerful wind tore the mountains apart and shattered the rocks before the LORD, but the LORD was not in the wind. After the wind there was an earthquake, but the LORD was not in the earthquake. After the earthquake came a fire, but the LORD was not in the fire. And after the fire came a gentle whisper.
1 Kings 19:11 – 12

I have not always paid attention to my life. To be honest, I only began paying close attention when I reached my early forties and found myself in a success panic. I was the president and CEO of a tremendously successful cable television company. I was fully engaged in a good and growing marriage. We had a son who was — there's no more appropriate way to say it — a prize.

And, of course, there was something gnawing at me. How was it that I could be so successful, so fortunate, and yet so frustratingly unfulfilled?

I knew perfectly well what I believed about business strategies and practices, family relationships, and the importance of friends. But I had not decided how I was going to reconcile all of these competing interests. And, as for the most important issue of all, my faith life, I knew what I believed, but I didn't really know what I planned to *do* about what I believed.

It was then that I started to wrestle with what I wanted out of the second half of my life. I was gripped with an unformed but very compelling idea that I should make my life truly productive, not merely profitable. Making a lot of money has its benefits, but what was I leaving behind that would make a difference in the world? Something was telling me that there was more to life than money. I began to reckon with the implications of the seasons of my life and to listen for the sound of the gentle stillness that breaks forth, unexpectedly, after the fire.

I began asking myself questions like these:

Am I listening for the still, small voice?

Is my work still the center of my life and identity?

Do I have an eternal perspective as a prism through which I view my life?

What is my truest purpose? My life work? My destiny?

What does it really mean to "have it all"?

What do I want to be remembered for?

What would my life look like if it really turned out well?

In the Scriptures, Jesus Christ taught that he had come to earth so that his followers might have abundant life, life to the fullest. That's a wonderful sentiment. And I think its point is missed by many people who think that religion is restrictive and forbidding, who think that Jesus came to scowl and scold and say, "No!" The Jesus I had come to know and love was leading me to the paths of a large life, not a small or narrow one. He was asking me to say a loud "Yes!" to a life packed with significance.

But I did not hear his yes in my first half because I was too busy to listen.

The issue for me was not belief. I was given the gift of belief in God at an early age. But for most of my first half, I was, to use a sports metaphor, stranded on second base. Consider the diagram on the next page, the concept of which first came to me from pastor and author Rick Warren.

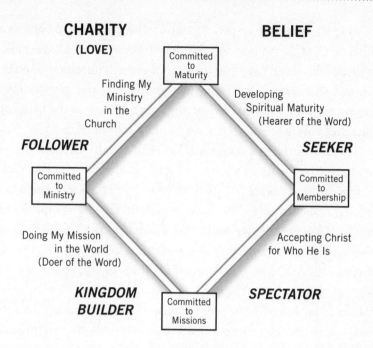

CHARITY
(LOVE)

BELIEF

Committed to Maturity

Finding My Ministry in the Church

Developing Spiritual Maturity (Hearer of the Word)

FOLLOWER

SEEKER

Committed to Ministry

Committed to Membership

Doing My Mission in the World (Doer of the Word)

Accepting Christ for Who He Is

KINGDOM BUILDER

SPECTATOR

Committed to Missions

First base is taking the simple, childlike step of belief, which is all that is required to become a member of God's family. For me it was a simple acceptance that what Jesus said about himself in the Bible was true. This step involves what Kierkegaard called "a leap of faith." Faith doesn't deny reason, but it is different than reason. It accepts, as a gift from God, a different set of capacities. Without faith we are spectators to affairs of the heart and soul. With faith we can go on to engage the other two capacities, our rational and emotional senses, on the journey of personal growth to second base.

For me the journey to second base was entirely about belief. It first engaged the heart and then the head. Rounding second base involved a shift from being what the Bible calls a "hearer of the Word" to being a "doer of the Word" — a shift from viewing faith as an internally held belief system to faith expressed in the form of loving behavior.

Like the majority of people who attend church and express a belief in God, I was comfortable standing on second base, making sure I believed the right things. I went to church on Sunday, listened to a sermon to strengthen my beliefs, and any "doing" was pretty much limited to putting some money in the offering plate and volunteering to teach a Sunday school class.

There is nothing wrong with belief. It's really the only thing God requires of us to receive his gift of eternal life. But God desires so much more for us than just right thinking. Faith expressed in behavior is "the most excellent way." Paul speaks of this in his great chapter on love, 1 Corinthians 13, which ends, "Now these three remain: faith, hope and love. But the greatest of these is love." The Greek word for love, *agape*, is exactly the same as the word for charity. Charity is the *expression* of love. It is as if faith and hope were acquired on the journey to second base in order to equip us for the second-half journey toward home base.

Third base involves becoming a follower by expressing our faith in the form of concrete action, usually in a religious setting, either a church or a parachurch organization. And then we are finally on the last stretch, the journey to home base. This stage involves making ourselves what Gordon MacDonald has called "kingdom builders." This means finding the mission in the world that has been specifically designed by God for each of us to do. It is what the Greeks called "destiny," what poet John Donne referred to when he said, "No man is an island, entire of itself."

The second half of the baseball diamond is about good works. It is not at all separate from the first half, which is about belief, but grows out of that belief and gives it integrity. Paraphrasing James's famous line, "Faith without works is dead," I would put it this way: "Faith without works dies." The life of faith must become a life of individual responsibility. The legs and hands must follow the heart and the head, or the body is not whole.

While God would like to see all of us hit a home run, most Christians never get beyond belief. A 2007 Gallup poll reported that 82 percent of Americans declare themselves to be Christians, which ought to be enough to infuse solid biblical values into all areas of culture. I do not doubt Gallup's findings, but I must tell you I do not see nearly that much evidence of Christian faith in our society. I believe that is because most of us are stuck somewhere between first and second base.

In the first half of life, there is barely enough time to go beyond second base. We are hunter-gatherers, doing our best to provide for our families, to advance our careers, and to pass our beliefs and values on to our children. In addition, for most men, and certainly a growing number of women, the first half finds us in our warrior mode. We need to prove to ourselves and others that we can accomplish something big, and the best way to do that is to become increasingly focused and intense.

I think of the first half as a season in which to develop faith and learn more about the unique way the Bible approaches life. The second half, when the pressure lets up, seems to be more the time when most people round second base and begin to *do* something about the faith they have developed. That's how it was for me.

In *The Odyssey*, the epic telling of the life of Odysseus, two great forces are pulling at Odysseus: work and home. He yearns to get home, yet he enjoys the battles along the way. Do you feel a kinship to him? During the first half, we too are pulled between the desire to be with our families and the adventure of trying to make it in our careers. Is it any wonder we do not hear that still, small voice calling us to something better?

The first half of life has to do with achieving and gaining, learning and earning. The majority do this in the most ordinary of ways: getting an education, entering the workforce, starting a family, buying a house, earning enough money to provide for needs as well as a few wants, setting goals, and climbing toward them. Some chase the prize in a more spectacular, aggressive fashion: closing a major deal, winning the big case, acquiring through leveraged buyouts and mergers, doing whatever it takes to make it to the top. Either way, few leave time in the first half for listening to God. If we have any spiritual interests, they usually take their form in typical first-half fashion: serving on the church building committee, teaching a Sunday school class, or organizing the annual stewardship campaign.

The second half is riskier because it has to do with living beyond the immediate. It is about releasing the seed of creativity and energy that has been implanted within us, watering and cultivating it so that we may be abundantly fruitful. It involves investing our gifts in service to others — and receiving the personal joy that comes as a result of that spending. This is the kind of risk for which entrepreneurs earn excellent returns much of the time.

True entrepreneurship is not foolhardy; nor does it require particular courage. It merely seeks to gather and examine as many of the facts as possible about the market and the environment that might impact a decision. And then a decision must quickly be made. Likewise, for the second half of life to be better than the first, you must make the choice to step outside of the safety of living on autopilot. You must wrestle with who you are, why you believe what you profess to believe about your life, and what you do to provide meaning and structure to your daily activities and relationships.

There is a risk in this decision: in tossing aside the security blanket that keeps you safe and warm in your cautiously controlled zone of comfort, you may have to set aside familiar markers and reference points. You may feel, at least at first, that you are losing control of your life.

To that I say, "Good for you."

It really is good for you to surrender control and, in the process, come more fully to your senses — those senses that enable you to be aware of life's adventures and rewards.

Your future, particularly in turbulent times such as these, is in great measure beyond your control, no matter how hard you try to nail it down or plan it out. This is true whatever season of life you find yourself passing through. Yet perhaps it is most resonant for those who are approaching their middle years, as I did when I was in my forties.

For me the transition into the afternoon of life was a time for reordering my time and my treasure, for reconfiguring my values and my vision of what life could be. It represented more than a renewal; it was a new beginning. It was more than a reality check; it was a fresh and leisurely look into the holiest chamber of my own heart, affording me, at last, an opportunity to respond to my soul's deepest longings.

And it was, as it turned out, a time to plant and a time to uproot, a time to weep and a time to laugh, a time to mourn and a time to dance, a time to search and a time to give up, a time to keep and a time to throw away. It has been the most important time in my life.

So far.

Writer and director Norman Corwin, now in his nineties, recalled his transition into middle age in the book *The Ageless Spirit*: "I remember now that the toughest birthday I ever faced was my fortieth. It was a big symbol because it said good-bye, good-bye, and good-bye to youth. But I think that when one has passed through that age it's like breaking the sound barrier."[1]

For it surely is a time to discover, as George Bernard Shaw had some years before, a taste of the "true joy" of life. He described it this way:

This is the true joy in life — the being used for a purpose

recognized by yourself as a mighty one, the being a force of nature instead of a feverish, selfish little clod of ailments and grievances, complaining that the world will not devote itself to making you happy. I am of the opinion that my life belongs to the whole community, and as long as I live, it is my privilege to do for it whatever I can. I want to be thoroughly used up when I die, for the harder I work, the more I live. I rejoice in life for its own sake. Life is no brief candle to me. It is a sort of splendid torch which I've got ahold of for the moment, and I want to make it burn as brightly as possible before handing it on to future generations.

In the introduction, I asked you to write your own epitaph to help you begin to think about your second half. Here's a question that will help you with the same goal: *If your life were absolutely perfect, how would it look to you?*

That's something worth mulling over for a good while, because the picture that will emerge is a snapshot that will help you find your bliss, your blessedness. But it will be an accurate picture only to the extent that you listen to the still, small voice within.

CHAPTER 2

The Hour of
Reverse Conversion

Some Christians know the precise moment of their conversion. The date, the day of the week, the hour, minute, second, nanosecond. *Boom!* In the twinkling of an eye, something happened, and they were changed ... born again ... forgiven ... saved.

That's not my story. I report this with neither regret nor pride. I was given the gift of faith at such an early age that I don't remember ever living without it. I have gone through my life with questions, to be sure, and the typical confusion about certain theological and doctrinal formulations, but I have never doubted God. I have always believed that Jesus is who he said he is.

I didn't achieve this state of trust and blissful assurance on my own. I didn't seek out the Lord. My unshaken faith is a gift from the Lord, the Lord who found *me*. So I can't recount a dramatic or emotional turning point in my spiritual development — save for a surprising reverse conversion experience I had at the age of fourteen, at which time I abandoned the notion I had had of becoming a clergyman, although in no way did I renounce my personal faith or commitments.

By my adolescent years, my family had moved from Oklahoma to Tyler, Texas, in the piney woods on the eastern side of the Lone Star State. My father, who was a hard-drinking hunter and Oklahoma state skeet shooting champion, had died when I was in the fifth grade, before we moved to Texas. I don't remember a great deal about him, although I do recall that he drank his whiskey straight from the bottle, in a manner, I was to learn later, all too common during those postwar days when Ernest Hemingway was writing great American books and rugged American men thought themselves to be tempered-tough and indestructible.

My father was not indestructible. He left a young widow and three small boys, and together we carried on. My mother continued running the radio station in Oklahoma for a brief time, and then we headed to Tyler to purchase and operate a radio station there.

My mother, suddenly on her own, developed into a visionary and successful media business executive. She filed an application for a license to operate the first television station in Tyler, competing against the owner of the local newspaper and against the most prominent philanthropic family in town, whose business, of course, was oil.

The odds against her were daunting. She was a widow, alone and relatively new in town, while the family of the local oil tycoon provided money and leadership for virtually every community charity and cause. And in nearby Dallas, the three television licenses had been granted to the owners of the area's newspapers.

Meanwhile, my mother had to go to a court in Smith County, Texas, to have her "disabilities" removed. At that time, in the early 1950s, state law prevented women from executing and signing contracts without their husbands unless a court declared them "femme sole," a legal designation that literally means "woman alone."

But despite the odds, and in the face of considerable cultural roadblocks, my mother persevered and was granted the license to operate KLTV in October of 1954. (The *L* stood for Lucille, my mother's first name.) Her determination and doggedness provided an important lesson for me, giving me an example of a can-do spirit and belief. At an early age, I came to believe that I too could accomplish almost anything through hard work and persistence.

My mother, who subsequently remarried twice with lamentable lack of success both times, lived for her business interests and her children. When she tucked me in bed at night, she didn't read Dr. Seuss books or Winnie-the-Pooh adventures. Instead, she taught me about balance sheets, depreciation schedules, and advertising sales strategies. And when she applied for the television station license, she told the Federal Communications Commission that she was seeking to acquire a station in the hope that her children would one day run the business.

My mother's single-mindedness and dedication produced both excitement and tension within me — a titanic, internal tug-of-war between leading a life of success in business and leading a life of service in ministry. I would not fully resolve this tension for decades, but I made a decisive turn at the age of fourteen.

I remember the moment with crystal clarity, the same way some people remember every detail of the circumstances surrounding their conversion experience or where they were when the World Trade Center was attacked on September 11, 2001.

My moment of vocational transformation took place in Miss Mittie Marsh's ninth-grade English class in Hogg Junior High School. Mittie Marsh was a legend in Tyler during my youth. She and her sisters, Minnie and Sarah, taught in the public schools in town and lived in a plantation-style mansion on South Broadway, the main street on which high school students cruised in their cars on Friday and Saturday nights. Mittie Marsh and her sisters set the standard for academic rigor in Tyler. They were the mentors who warned you, "If you don't get it right, you won't get into the college you want to go to."

I was seated in the second row on the far left side of the classroom. To this day I'm still not certain what prompted the decision, but it was in that spot that — *Pow!* — I somehow knew instantly that preaching, baptizing, marrying, and burying were out, and making money as a TV executive was in. I had made a clearheaded, teenaged decision to put myself in the driver's seat of a turbocharged car.

Of course, "clearheaded" and "teenaged" are terms rarely seen on the same page, much less linked in the same clause, and television, then in its early infancy, scarcely looked to be a serious threat to the long-established American entertainment habits of reading, conversing, and listening to the radio. But what did I know? I was just in junior high, barely blossoming in the spring of my life. The world of business — and particularly the new and exciting technology of television — appeared to be a fabulous sport, with greater drama and spoils than I could imagine.

And, quite frankly, I wanted to be the guy who stepped to the plate and slugged the game-winning home run in the bottom of the ninth inning. Decisive. Heroic. It was a momentous choice that would pave the way for seasons still to come.

I still love the sport of the television business — the competition, the strategies, the conquests. One executive I knew (who later committed suicide) called business "the world's greatest sport." I know exactly what he meant, because I too once found it indescribably exhilarating to measure the competition, to run up the score, to win, win, win. I still find it enlivening to be a player of consequence. As well, I believe that human organizations provide the best learning environment and greatest intellectual challenge, much more so than memorizing facts from a book. What we learn formally is best enhanced through experience, and my experience in the television business has taught me a great deal about what it takes to be a winner in the success game.

But now I recognize that there are other games, played on

many fields. And I've learned that there are ways to win besides dominating the ratings race and piling up the score through increased market share or burgeoning profits.

That valuable lesson was disclosed to me — as perhaps it already has been, or likely will be one day, to you — slowly, through uncomplicated attention-paying and the simple seasoning of the passages of life. It began to sink into my heart — and seep into the space where my decisions were being made — in significant ways about three decades ago, when I was doing great things in business, and little else. It was the genesis of a steady and thoughtful reexamination of the stunning reverse conversion experience that had come to me in a flash in that junior high school classroom, where clearheaded dreams were launched in the fog of youth.

I began to think about what I would do about what I believed.

CHAPTER 3

A Season of Searching and Self-Help

There is a time for everything ...
a time to search and a time to give up.
Ecclesiastes 3:1, 6

I t's a cherished tenet of supply-side economics that a rising tide lifts all the boats in the ocean. Not everyone subscribes to that theory. But my industry, the television business, was nothing short of a commercial and cultural tidal wave that rolled across the United States during the 1960s and 1970s. It became an entertainment and information colossus, changing the way people behaved and related to each other.

My boat rose.

Walter Cronkite, legendary news anchor for CBS, emerged not only as a household name and familiar face, but also ranked high on a list of the most trusted men in America. Because of television's power to confer authority and celebrity, that's the way it was — and largely still is, even with the proliferation of voices from cable, satellite, and the Internet.

It was, as you well might imagine, an especially fortuitous and rewarding time to be in the commercial television business. Over a three-decade period, in which my family's holdings expanded from a single TV station in Tyler to an array of cable television systems in several parts of the country, Buford Television, Inc., grew at a rate of 25 percent annually.

I learned many years ago from management expert Peter Drucker that for business growth to be sustained year after year, the leaders of a company have to be crazy, crooked, or open to change based on their company's growth and the opportunities and challenges that expansion poses for them. Well, the television business gave us a wonderful ride from 1954 to 1986. Very few industries have had a period of uninterrupted growth such as those of us in television management experienced during that time.

But the solid, even spectacular, growth of Buford Television, Inc., depended in some measure on judicious change. By the mid-1980s, for example, the action was no longer in owning individual stations. In those days, most people in the United States had the option of watching thirty-five to fifty-five channels through cable television. At BTI, we divested our television stations and moved entirely into the cable business. Today, of course, we have hundreds of video, audio, and text options available not only through our television sets but also via our computers and wireless phones.

Business, like life, is seasonal. Circumstances change. A company, just like a person, needs to periodically shift its focus in order to achieve healthy growth.

I still recall the colorful early days of ABC-TV's *Monday Night Football* broadcasts, when "Dandy" Don Meredith, a former quarterback for the Dallas Cowboys, would signal to the audience that the game was done, even if there were several minutes remaining to be played. "Turn out the lights," he would sing in his Texas twang, "the party's over." Although I appreciate the wisdom in the old proverb that it's better to be lucky than smart, I believe that it's best of all to be bright enough to know when the party's over and when it's time to move on to the next event.

I moved into the presidency and chairman's seat in the

company and became the oldest family member at the age of thirty-one, when my mother died in a fire that consumed her hotel room in downtown Dallas. My mother had taught me a great deal about business and about life. She was, like most people of achievement, a person of great strengths and also great weaknesses.

She was a risk taker and was forceful, dedicated to success in business and to raising me with the gifts of self-esteem and self-assurance. When I was in high school, she introduced me wherever we went as "the world's greatest left end." The truth was that I played on the second string in my junior year, backing up a truly fine, all-state left end. In my senior year, I started in that position but was merely adequate as a football player. Still, I loved hearing her introduce me that way, and those words gave me both affirmation and inspiration.

But my mother was also naive and often undisciplined — weaknesses that no doubt contributed greatly to the disappointments and dissolution of her later marital relationships. They were weaknesses I swore to avoid.

Although I had worked in the family business since leaving college, my mother's death signaled a new season in my life — new responsibilities, new choices, new dreams. It was time for the next generation, and it came during an era of enormous upheaval in society. The leading edge of the baby boomers was entering college and the workforce. The Vietnam War was dragging on. Richard Nixon was plotting his reelection, and Watergate was waiting to happen.

I was not unaffected by all that social straining, but my chief focus was on growing the business and myself. I was deeply attracted to self-help and self-improvement books and tapes at the time. I read everything Peter Drucker had written. I attended the American Management Association's Presidents' Course. I went to the Harvard Business School's Owner/Manager Program — a nine-week hothouse course that compressed major elements of their MBA curriculum.

Without benefit of the "mind-expanding" drugs that were popular at the time, I visualized my dreams. What I could conjure and believe, I knew I could achieve with a concerted effort of the will. That was my credo, my mantra. Tune out Woodstock and forget about White House dirty tricks and the trustworthiness of anyone over the age of thirty. I firmly believed I could shape my life by my dreams and the desires of my heart.

The only piece of my personality that gave me even a moment's pause was a fleeting concern about my degree of intensity and drivenness about the business. I had a sense that this hyperfocus might cost me in other areas of my life. Through all the excitement of actually running a business and reaping the rewards of success, a question tugged at a corner of my mind: *What might you lose with all this gaining?* Clearly, there was more to life than business.

Even so, not long after taking over the business, I hid myself away with a yellow pad and embarked on a painstaking career and personal evaluation that would allow course corrections.

I asked myself the question I posed to you in chapter 1: If my life were absolutely perfect, what would its elements be?

I was thirty-four years old at the time, and it was the first opportunity I had taken in my life to reflect deeply on what I most wanted to accomplish and be. The answers would provide a glimpse of how I should live. I wrote down six goals:

To grow the business at least 10 percent a year.

To have a vital marriage to my wife, Linda, and to remain married to her until death temporarily forced us apart.

To serve God by serving others — to lay up treasure in heaven by teaching or counseling in my spare time at the church we attended or anywhere else where I was allowed and encouraged to use my gifts.

To engender high self-esteem in our son, Ross. This, I believed, would best equip him for whatever circumstances he found himself in. I ranked myself as a father not so much on his grades or whether he won tennis tournaments, but rather on whether my son felt good about himself. An important part of this was instilling a grounded faith in something trustworthy beyond himself.

To grow culturally and intellectually in ways that had somehow evaded me during my student years.

To figure out what to do with the money I was making and to determine how much was enough. I determined to invest the money I didn't use or didn't need in the highest cause I could imagine. What would that be?

These six goals were the way I made sense of what I was doing with my life. I focused almost exclusively on these areas and eliminated anything that didn't fit. The big change from my prior intense focus on growing the business was that I had introduced an element of balance into my life: the last five goals defined what was important to me. They answered the question, "What will I lose with all this gaining?" I wanted to be sure I didn't trade something I considered priceless — the love of my wife, the self-esteem of my son, the opportunity to broaden my horizons through learning, the expression of my faith through a life of service — for something I had come to have more than enough of: money, power, and achievement.

That was not, neither then nor now, an exhaustive list of life goals. But it was enough to get me into a search for the core commitments and passions that could help me make sense of myself.

I was a first-half player who was beginning to see the second half coming.

CHAPTER 4

Success Panic

It snuck in like a thief in the night — a quiet, insidious intruder disturbing the dark peace and slinking about to pick at the trappings of a life overflowing with contentment, money, achievement, and energy.

"Success panic" passed through the threshold of my door when I was forty-four. It hit me with a blunt object — my slavish devotion to the art of the deal and the thrill of the kill. How much was enough?

By this time, the television business had grown beyond our most optimistic projections. As a result, I had long since arrived at — and, in fact, surpassed — the goals I had established for accumulation of wealth. I had the big house. I had the Jaguar. I could, and did, travel to any place on earth I wished. I had either reached or was ahead of the plan to meet most of the rest of my goals as well.

Success panic was wholly unexpected. I remember reading a Sierra Club book about the assault on the western ridge of Mount Everest. After spending millions of dollars and experiencing loss of life among their fellow climbers, two men finally reached the peak of Mount Everest. There, at the top, they viewed the world from its highest point. They had overcome enormous impediments to reach their destination, their ultimate goal, yet the emotion they experienced was not one of unadulterated elation and joyfulness. After just a few minutes, one of them began worrying about how to get down the other side before the wind blew them off the top of the mountain.

In the first-half mind-set, getting to the apex is far more exciting and rewarding than arriving.

When success panic struck, it brought me to a long-delayed crossroads and forced me to consider a critically important set of decisions before I could take another step:

> Would I move the finish line forward so that I could keep running the race and measuring the time it took to complete each new lap?
>
> Would I give myself permission to be open to new possibilities?
>
> Could I have a constructive midlife crisis?
>
> After success, what?

These were difficult questions for me to address because of my attachment to business and my awareness of the entrepreneurial and leadership qualities that I had developed through my professional career. The business arena was the venue where I proved myself — my worth, my wisdom — each day; it was a stage on which I could demonstrate my gifts and my savvy. It was a comfortable world for me, not merely because it was familiar, but also because it was a world that expected me to be demanding and not loving. It was measurable.

I was, frankly, frightened by the idea of turning back toward the work of the church or works of service — those long-ago but not-quite-forgotten promptings toward ministry that had gripped me as a child. Ministry — as I always had understood it — was loving but not very demanding — the very antithesis of the real world I had lived in quite cheerfully for nearly a quarter century. It seemed too squishy, too nice, too otherworldly, too difficult to measure.

What's more, all my friends provided ample affirmation for

me to remain as the CEO of a successful company. Yet, just as it was with Elijah, the still, small voice — barely audible, always gentle — kept calling to me as I was sitting there in a cold, middle-aged sweat brought on by the still-roaring flames of my success. The gentle but insistent voice was asking me to consider — what else? — a question that I had deferred and suppressed for all of my adult life: *Do you understand the difference between being called and being driven?*

Quite plainly, I had come to a point at which yet another fundamental decision had to be made. Like most decisions in real life, it was not a stark choice between black and white, between self-indulgence and self-denial, between leadership and follow-ship; it could be found in the vast gray area between such polar extremes. But facing that question only served to underscore both the price and the glory of making a commitment to put my most central beliefs and tested talents into action in my life.

It was another helpful episode in my search for meaning, one that softened me up for the imminent exploration within, the probing that would finally help me unveil the source of my satisfaction and longings. For it was the question that made me wonder what I might be losing with all this gaining.

My worry was that I would become addicted to success. The interface between success and significance is a delicate and dangerous zone — one garners as much success as possible without getting captured by it, becoming its prisoner. Keeping success the servant, not the master. It's a tension very much like the scene in the popular movie from the 1980s, *Fatal Attraction*, where Michael Douglas is sitting across from Glenn Close, knowing that his wife is going to be gone for the weekend and feeling crazy with desire. He is right on the border between being master of his desire and committing an act that would make him its prisoner.

He chose to become a prisoner, and I knew it was time to make my own choice.

CHAPTER 5

Locating the Mainspring

In my hour of deepest need, grace led me to an atheist.

Mike Kami is a strategic planning consultant. He is brilliant, demanding, and intuitive. He slices through all the pretense and posturing, and hones in on the core. A top resource consultant for the American Management Association, Kami was, at one time, director of strategic planning for IBM, serving that company during its years of rapid growth. He was then hired away by Xerox for a seven-figure bonus to do the same thing for them. He is independent, iconoclastic, and ruthless in his analysis.

He does not believe in God, but I can testify that — at least in my life — God worked unmistakably through Mike Kami.

I was accustomed to putting together periodic strategic plans for my business. These plans served as a yardstick by which those of us in the company could measure our effectiveness in bringing our common dreams to fruition. They were easy to flesh out and, most of the time, fun to execute.

But this was substantially different. Now I needed to draw up a strategic plan for *me*. So I spread out my jumbled dreams and desires, lists of perceived strengths and weaknesses, professions of faith, projects begun and half begun, things to do and things to abandon. It was a quagmire of both complementary and conflicting ambitions, a cacophony of noisy themes and trills of the sort one hears when symphony orchestra musicians are warming up for performance and seeking their pitch.

What should I do? How could I be most useful? Where should

I invest my own talents, time, and treasure? What are the values that give purpose to my life? What is the overarching vision that shapes me? Who am I? Where am I? Where am I going? How do I get there?

In this blizzard of wonderment, Mike Kami asked me a simple and penetrating question: *"What's in the box?"*

When I asked him to explain, Mike related an experience he had had in the 1980s with a group of Coca-Cola executives and their plan to introduce "New Coke." The corporate leaders told Mike that the mainspring and driving force of their business was "great taste." They conducted numerous taste tests, found a new formula that tasted better than the original Coca-Cola, introduced "New Coke" shortly thereafter — and promptly stepped into one of the biggest marketing debacles of all time.

They called Mike back in for another planning session. "You must have put the wrong word in the box," Mike told them. "Let's try again." After several hours, they found something else to put in the box: "American tradition."

The executives had recognized that pulling Coca-Cola from the market was akin to tampering with an American institution like motherhood or apple pie. Finding the right word to put in the box — identifying their core mission — enabled the company to recover its momentum quickly after a monumental blunder.

For my part, as I was searching for the right word to put in the box, I explained to Kami that I was open to fresh endeavors and new possibilities. I told him that I had gradually come to see that I really didn't have to be a religious professional or an ordained minister to live out my Christian convictions, and I warned him that I was serious about shifting at least some of my energy away from business pursuits into the direction of some unspecified realm of "service." It was probably a warning to me as well.

Well, Kami took me at my word. He announced that we could

not put together an honest plan for my life until I identified the mainspring. "I've been listening to you for a couple of hours," he said, "and I'm going to ask you what's in the box. For you, it is either money or Jesus Christ. If you can tell me which it is, I can tell you the strategic planning implications of that choice. If you can't tell me, you are going to oscillate between those two values and be confused."

No one had ever put such a significant question to me so directly. After a few minutes (which seemed like hours), I said, "Well, if it has to be one or the other, I'll put Jesus Christ in the box."

It was an act of faith, and it was a daunting challenge to me to be open to change and adventure. Even more than that, *it was a commitment to do something about the faith I already had.* By acknowledging Christ as my guiding light, I had invoked the promise that he would direct my paths, no matter where they took me.

Our planning session was conducted at a beautiful spot in California. My wife, Linda, was with us so that she could be involved in the discussions and planning. Neither one of us knew fully what we were getting ourselves into, and both of us were considerably apprehensive.

Kami pushed us hard — and successfully. To put Christ in the box, I found, is actually a sign of contradiction, a paradox. To put Christ in the box is to break down the walls of the box and allow the power and grace of his life to invade every aspect of your own life. It follows the same wonderfully inverted logic as the ancient assertion that it is in giving that one receives, in our weakness we are made strong, and in dying we are born to richer life.

I had chosen to make Christ my primary loyalty but not my exclusive loyalty. That was an important distinction, for I still had loyalties to Linda, to work, to friends, and to projects. Christ is the center of all that, but he would not stand in the way of those other things that give me balance and wholeness.

For me the logic of this allegiance led me to stay involved with my business, functioning as a rear-echelon chairman of the board and devoting about 20 percent of my time to setting the vision and values of the company, picking key executives, setting standards, and monitoring performance. The remaining 80 percent of my time was given over to an array of other things, most of which center on leadership training for churches and nonprofit organizations — serving those who serve others, helping them be more effective in their work.

Let me be honest about this: I still have a penthouse in the city, a country home at the East Texas farm, and a new Lexus. I do not believe it is in keeping with my "calling" to assume a diametrically different lifestyle from the one I have enjoyed throughout my life. Many people avoid taking the risk for a better second half because they mistakenly think it necessitates a drastic change. But I believe God gave me a gift to create wealth and enjoy its benefits, including the joy of using it to help others.

Related to this, what we *do* with what we believe grows out of our own history, and my history was neither missionary nor monastic. I truly believe that God uses people in their areas of strength and is unlikely to send us into areas in which we are likely to be amateurs and incompetents.

I realize that not everyone can afford to devote only 20 percent of his or her time to a career. I am fortunate in that respect. But don't let the fact that you have to work for a living limit the grace God has in store for you during your second half. Don't allow the second half of your life to be characterized by decline, boredom, and increasing ineffectiveness for the kingdom.

Listen carefully to that still, small voice, and then do some honest soul searching. What's in *your* box? Is it money? Career? Family? Freedom?

Remember, you can only have one thing in the box. Regardless of your position in life, once you have identified what's in your box, you will be able to see the cluster of activities — surrounded by quiet times for spiritual disciplines, reading, and reflecting — that put into play your "one thing" and keep you growing.

But be careful. Growth is not always easy.

CHAPTER 6

"Adios, Ross"

There I was, sailing happily through my constructive midlife crisis, hoisting my "one thing" up the mast into place, spinnaker billowing in the balmy breeze.

Then, without warning, along came a rogue wave that blew the boat over.

I had gone through life more or less comfortable with the idea that there are some things you know, some things you suspect, and some things you're just never going to understand. No less an authority than Aristotle spoke to that when he said that the soul operates on two levels: the rational, which takes in what can be seen and measured, and the sphere beyond the rational, which defies human comprehension and belongs in the realm of the gods.

But this new development threatened to plunge me into yet another dimension: the realm of the despondent.

My son, Ross — our only child — was a person of great promise. He was my heir, my successor, and in ways that may seem odd to you but absolutely real to me, one of my greatest heroes.

After Ross graduated from Texas Christian University in Fort Worth, he moved to Denver to take a job as an investment banker. He was preparing for the time when he would come back to Texas to join the family business and eventually take a leadership position in it. He made $150,000 his first full year of work in the deal-making business, and his second year — only barely begun — would likely have sent his income soaring to over

$500,000. There was big money to be made in his line of work in the late 1980s. But far more important than his financial successes, Ross was a good human being — determined, energetic, caring — with wonderful people skills. He had many friends, and he loved life in all its pleasures and ambiguities.

On the evening of January 3, 1987, I received a call from my brother Jeff, who told me that Ross and two of his friends had attempted to swim the Rio Grande River, which separates South Texas from Mexico.

"I think we have serious trouble," Jeff told me in a voice that meant it. "Ross is missing in the Rio Grande."

It was a lark that led the three young men to the Rio Grande: they wanted to experience what it was like for illegal aliens to cross the watery border into a land of promise. Ross was twenty-four years old, and it was the last adventure of his life on earth.

My brother informed me that the Texas Rangers were coordinating the search for Ross and one of his companions; the third young man was alive and frantic about the fate of his friends. I flew down to the Rio Grande Valley to join in the search, arriving by daybreak the next morning. I hired airplanes, helicopters, boats, trackers with dogs — everything money could buy.

By three o'clock in the afternoon, I looked into the eyes of one of the trackers and knew that I would never see Ross again in this life.

I remember walking along a limestone bluff perhaps two hundred feet above the muddy and treacherous river, as frightened as I've ever felt. *Here's something you can't dream your way out of,* I told myself. *Here's something you can't think your way out of, buy your way out of, or work your way out of.* It was all too clear in this maddening solitude on the river bluff. *This is,* I thought, *something you can only trust your way out of.*

The incomprehensible was breaking out all around me, and there was no way I could understand it apart from an eternal perspective. Albert Einstein once said that "what is incomprehensible is beyond the realm of science. It is in the realm of God." This was truly in the realm of God.

I remember sending up a prayer that, in retrospect, seems to be the most intelligent petition I ever made to Heaven. "Dear God," I pleaded, "somehow give me the ability to accept and absorb whatever grace people might bring to me at this terrible time. Amen."

The search for Ross and his friend continued, and grace abounded in my life and relationships. They found Ross's body in the spring, more than four months later, about ten miles downriver. Before his body was recovered, we had found on his desk at home in Denver a handwritten copy of his will, dated February 20, 1986, less than a year before the river swallowed his body. Through that long winter of fear and uncertainty, his words were also a grace to me.

"Well, if you're reading my will, then, obviously, I'm dead," Ross began. "I wonder how I died? Probably suddenly, because otherwise I would have taken the time to rewrite this. Even if I am dead, I think one thing should be remembered, and that is that I had a great time along the way. More importantly, it should be noted that I am in a better place now."

The will directed how he wanted his earthly goods distributed, and Ross concluded the document with this benediction: "In closing, I loved you all and thank you. You've made it a great life. Make sure you all go up instead of down, and I'll be waiting for you at heaven's gate. Just look for the guy in the old khakis, Stetson, and faded shirt, wearing a pair of Ray-Bans and a Jack Nicholson smile. I also thank God for giving me the chance to write this before I departed. Thanks. Adios, Ross."

As horrifying and sad as it was, and is, to have lost him, Ross's disappearance and death also provided the greatest moments of rare insight and grandest gestures of immeasurable grace and joy that I ever hope to experience. Utter emptiness and brokenness left me feeling awful and wonderful at the same time. Close and silent embraces from friends, letters and phone calls of concern and empathy, and gifts of meals prepared and brought to our home were much-needed signs of love. One letter in particular showed us just how much Ross's life had been a witness to those around him:

> *Dear Mr. and Mrs. Buford,*
>
> *Ross and I were best friends. All that he had, Ross shared with me. He shared his thoughts and ideas, his pleasures and his pains; he shared a whole lot of laughter. But most of all, he shared his love.*
>
> *Well, now Ross has a new best friend. And now Ross is with his new best friend. But just as before, Ross continues to share. Today Ross is sharing his new best friend with his old best friend.*
>
> *I thank the Lord God for Ross, and I thank Ross for the Lord God.*
>
> *Ronnie*

Despite the comfort of those words, I was forced to lean on God entirely in those dark weeks after Ross's death. I often thought of the Scripture verse "Trust in the LORD with all your heart and lean not on your own understanding." I learned that God truly is sufficient and that his strength is made perfect in weakness. I learned that in my life on earth, I live as one who is on an adventure that could end at any moment. I am not in control!

There is a simple Quaker prayer about giving and receiving that I uttered the night after I lost Ross and that I pray often to this day. Because the Quakers use their hands as a type of religious artifact or symbol, the first part of the prayer is done with your palms up, visualizing yourself receiving all that you need from God. The second part is prayed with palms down, visualizing all your cares and concerns being left in the lap of a benevolent and loving God.

I used this physical prayer when I spoke at a church two and a half weeks after we buried Ross.

"God," I began, "you have given my life into my hands. I give it back to you. My time, my property, my life itself … knowing it is only an instant compared to my life with you (and with Ross) in eternity."

With palms down, I concluded, "Father, to you I release the cares and concerns of this world, knowing you loved me enough to give your only Son in my behalf. I'm a sinner in need of a Savior and, once again, I accept what you have done for me as sufficient. In Jesus' name. Amen."

In his letter to the Romans, the apostle Paul wrote a comforting message that has encouraged millions of troubled, despondent, broken believers over the centuries: "We know that God causes all things to work together for good to those who love God, to those who are called according to His purpose" (8:28 NASB). All things really do work together, but not without an eternal perspective.

I live in two worlds. One is the world of distraction and busyness. It's the world of deal making and score keeping, of stock market booms and busts. That world is like a cloud; it's going to perish. The other world I live in is where Ross is now — the world of the eternal. And it's the reality of that latter world that allows me to respond, with confidence: "Adios, Ross, *for now*."

This eternal perspective has made me return, with soaring consolation, to George Bernard Shaw's eloquent passion for life and the responsibility to use it up each day. "I rejoice in life for its own sake," Shaw said in an address in 1907. "Life is no brief candle to me. It's a sort of splendid torch which I've got hold of for the moment, and I want to make it burn as brightly as possible before handing it on to the future generations."

One reason I place my dear Ross on a short list of great heroes is because he was, despite the few years of his life, no brief candle. He was a splendid torch — vital, charismatic, magnetic, attractive — full of the attributes that all of us wish we had in greater abundance. Ross used his gifts to the full each day. He didn't shortchange himself, even though his days among us were so few. Ross's death, while tragic, was an inspiration to me to burn brightly while it is day.

The famous English poet John Donne once wrote, "No man is an island, entire of itself; every man is a piece of the continent, a part of the main.... Any man's death diminishes me, because I am involved in mankind; and therefore never send to know for whom the bell tolls; it tolls for thee."[1]

Allow yourself to listen for the bell. And before it tolls for you, allow it to be your wake-up call.

PART 2

HALFTIME

The thing is to understand myself, to see what God really wishes me to do ... to find the idea for which I can live and die.

Søren Kierkegaard

CHAPTER 7

Taking Stock

I have often said that the sole cause of man's unhappiness is that he does not know how to stay quietly in his room.... What people want is not the easy peaceful life that allows us to think of our unhappy condition, nor the dangers of war, nor the burdens of office, but the agitation that takes our mind off it and diverts us. That is why we prefer the hunt to the capture. That is why men are so fond of hustle and bustle; that is why prison is such a fearful punishment; that is why the pleasures of solitude are so incomprehensible.

Pascal, *Pensées*

My father was a hunter. My son was a hunter too. The genetic package that triggered the primal outdoor sportsman impulse within the two of them must have skipped a generational beat. I happen to be a gamesman, preferring sports in which the results can be more readily measured and in which a time clock is either an ally or an opponent. I lean toward football, in which you tally up statistics after each quarter, or the sport of business, in which the bottom line is examined at the end of each quarter. At the end of both games, you have a final score.

I like keeping score.

Nevertheless, Pascal was right — many of us do prefer the hunt to the capture. We find greater satisfaction from the thrill of the chase than from the successful completion of the conquest. Burying ourselves in the hustle and bustle of daily existence, we rarely take time out to experience the wonder and stillness of solitude, where the quiet voice of God is most audible.

"If I were a doctor and were asked for my advice," theologian and philosopher Søren Kierkegaard once said, "I should reply: Create silence."

Halftime cannot be a noisy place.

The first half is noisy, busy, almost frenetic. It is not that you do not *want* to listen for that still, small voice. It's just that you never seem to have time to do it. Try to reconstruct your daily schedule from the past two weeks. Chances are, you will not even be able to remember what you did yesterday, let alone two weeks ago. If you pull out your calendar, however, you'll discover why — you simply had so many things on your plate it would be impossible to remember them all.

Were all of these activities important? Were they the types of things you would die for? Are you looking forward to more of the same? The expectation that work would provide more than a paycheck, that it would add meaning to life, has provoked an epidemic of dislocating and dispiriting midlife crises for many American workers. Millions of people enter their forties feeling not that they are at the pinnacle of their power or at the top of their career, but that they are trapped. Trapped in a job that rarely challenges them. Trapped in relationships that are stagnant if not destructive. Trapped in the consequences of choices made a generation earlier.

For several years Harvard Business School held an interesting workshop called Age of Options that was designed for people in halftime. The purpose of this workshop was to ensure participants "that their next career phase [was] fulfilling and imbued with purpose." It helped participants "reassess their career development paths and define future choices in terms of personal needs and inclinations."[1] I mention this to emphasize how prevalent this need is in our culture. As each generation begins hitting forty, more and more people will be entering halftime.

It is not unnatural nor should it overly concern you that you feel the need for a change. The mistake most people make when they begin to feel this way is to ignore the voice that is telling them to stop and listen. And there are many ways to ignore it. Some simply bear down, reasoning that they need more discipline, more focus. Some turn to diversions, both healthy and reckless. Most, I am convinced, enter a sort of sleepwalking stage during which they force themselves to hold on until retirement. None of these approaches will make your second half better than the first, and they may, in fact, make it worse.

If you are hearing a voice speak softly to you, it is time to head for the locker room, catch your breath, and get ready for the second half — a better second half than the first. For a football coach and his team, this is the time to take stock, to look back on what was accomplished. What worked? What didn't? Plays that didn't work can either be adjusted or dropped for the second half; new plays can be drawn up and inserted. Many times a good second half depends on what is done during halftime.

As you take stock, ask yourself these similar questions: What is my passion? How am I wired? Where do I belong? What do I believe? What will I do about what I believe? Or, as Peter Drucker advised people who were looking for their life's task: What are my values, my aspirations, my directions, and what do I have to do, to learn, to change, in order to make myself capable of living up to my demands on myself and my expectations of life?

While I cannot tell you exactly how to answer those questions, I can share — in the form of general concepts — what worked best for me as I prepared to go back out onto the field.

Make peace. Too many people approach the second half of

their lives with regrets over the first half. ("I should have spent more time with my family." "I should have developed better relationships." "I should have …") Regret is a tough emotion to live down: it haunts you in ways that will sap your strength and inspiration to go on to better things. So, one of the first things you need to do in halftime is make peace with your first-half set of issues.

This doesn't mean that you are proud of all you've done or that you would change nothing in your life if you could. Any honest look back will recall several things you wish you would have done differently. The key is to keep these things in perspective and accept them as an inevitable part of growth.

A friend of mine recalls having regrets about how he raised his son. He expressed those regrets to a family acquaintance and took great comfort in this reply: "It doesn't help much to dwell on those things you did or didn't do in the past. At the time, you did the very best you could, given your knowledge and experience. You did not intentionally do anything to disappoint your son, even though now that you have the benefit of a few years' experience, you can see how you might have done things differently. Don't blame yourself for good intentions that might have been applied improperly."

Since you cannot go back and undo past mistakes, you really have only two options. You can dwell on them and become consumed with the effects they may have had on your family and career. Or you can come to terms with them through grace, accepting them as poignant markers from which you can learn something valuable for the second half. Halftime is not about beating yourself up for what you did not do, but for coming to terms with your failures and recognizing that you live under grace.

Take time. The biggest mistake most of us make in the first half is not taking enough time for the things that are really important. So when you enter your halftime, you need to make sure you don't repeat that mistake. Naturally, this requires a certain amount of discipline and time management, and you may tend to view this as yet another appointment in your already overscheduled planner. But you would not be heading into halftime if you were not serious about making changes in your life.

A while ago I had the pleasure of meeting Konosuke Matsushita, chairman of the huge and highly successful Japanese electronics company bearing his last name. Matsushita follows the practice, not uncommon in Asia, of retreating to his garden from time to time in order to live a contemplative and reflective life. When Matsushita walks into a room, the awe is palpable. Without saying a word, he bespeaks a powerful centeredness and elegant reserve.

I am a big believer in getting away from the crowd for a period of time to do some halftime thinking. A distinctive of my second half is that I set aside time for introspection almost every weekend. My few hours of uninterrupted reading and thinking are the wellspring from which I draw living water to nurture the activities of the rest of my week. For you, this could be anything from getting up an hour earlier and doing some quiet meditating to spending a long weekend at a hotel in another city.

It may have taken you twenty years or more to get to halftime. Don't expect to solve all your first-half issues and plan for the second half in a few hours. For most people, halftime spreads out over several months, even years. But it will never happen if we don't give it the time it deserves.

Be deliberate. Halftime is more than putting your feet up and meditating. It's more than time away to think, pray, and play. A successful halftime needs some structure. Set an agenda that will help you "walk" through the important issues. Such an agenda will indeed include time to pray and listen, to read the Scriptures, and to think. But it should also include some deliberate questions. The following list may help you get started:

Am I missing anything in my life right now that's important to me?

What am I passionate about?

Who am I?

What do I value?

What do I want to be doing in ten years? In twenty?

What gifts has God given me that have been perfected over time?

What gifts has he given me that I am unable to use?

What would I be willing to die for?

What is it about my job that makes me feel trapped?

What realistic changes can I make in my employment?

Would I be willing to take a less stressful (and lower-paying) job to be happier — to be closer to my true self?

What steps do I need to take tomorrow to have a second half that is better than my first half?

You might consider writing your answers in a notebook or diary. I am engaged each day in writing a kind of spiritual autobiography — the sacred story of my very human existence, the relentless search for the most noble, decent part of me. If this seems a bit self-indulgent and prideful, it is because you still have one foot in the first half. Your "one thing" is still locked away in your heart's holiest chamber. Open your heart and let the answers spill out onto the pages of your own story.

Share the journey. I cannot imagine making the transition from the first half to the second without being accompanied on the journey by my wife. Linda was with me when I was forced to put either a dollar sign or a cross in the box that represented what was most important in my life. She did not flinch when I drew the cross, but she did not remain a silent partner. She asked questions, made suggestions, kept me honest. If your marriage is truly a partnership (which I believe it ought to be), it would be wrong for you to impose a whole new lifestyle without first consulting your spouse.

Be honest. Some people make the mistake of using halftime to fantasize, wistfully projecting various images of themselves into unrealistic situations that will never happen. In any other setting it's called daydreaming, and it's not a bad thing to do on your way home from work. But getting ready for a better second half is not daydreaming. You need to honestly face the tough, nitty-gritty questions about finances, other family members, long-range goals, and so on. And when you *do* ask the hard questions, don't fudge on the answers. To make the second half better than the first, you need to discover the real you. For much of the first half, you had to be someone else. That's not duplicity, it's just the reality for all of us as we climb the ladder. Your second-half self is your genuine self, so be honest enough to discover it.

Be patient. It took you the better part of two decades to reach this point. You can't undo everything overnight. You will still have to go to work tomorrow. Bills will arrive in the mail. Clients will expect to have their calls returned. And a clear picture of what you should do with the rest of your life may not emerge anytime soon — or may not emerge at all.

Have faith. For Christians, halftime is basically a time to answer the question, "What will I do about what I believe?" Begin to answer that by putting faith to work but trusting God to guide you. Listen to his voice through Scripture, and listen to the thoughts he places in your mind when you talk with him. To someone accustomed to listening to consultants, superiors, subordinates, and market research, this might be hard to do. Listen and trust.

Halftime Drill

Answer the following questions to help you take stock of your
first half as you prepare for a better second half. Be honest, and
write down your answers.

1. What do I want to be remembered for?
    Write a description of how your life would look if it
        turned out just the way you wished.

2. What about money?
    How much is enough?
    If I have more than enough, what purpose do I serve with
        the excess?
    If I have less than enough, what am I willing to do to
        correct that?

3. How am I feeling about my career now?
    Is this what I want to be doing with my life ten years from
        now?

4. Am I living a balanced life?
    What are the important elements in my life that deserve
        more time?

5. What is the primary loyalty in my life?

6. Where do I look for inspiration, mentors, and working
    models for my second half?

7. Peter Drucker said that two important needs are self-
    realization and community. On a scale of 1 to 10 (10 being
    the highest), how am I doing in these areas?

8. Draw a line that describes the ups and downs of your life.
    Or draw three lines, one for personal life, one for family life,
    and one for work life. Where do they intersect? Where do
    they diverge?

9. Which of the following transition options seems to fit my
    temperament and gifts best? (Evaluate each option on a scale
    of 1 to 10.)

a. Keep on doing what I already do well, but change the environment.
b. Change the work but stay in the same environment.
c. Turn an avocation into a new career.
d. Double-track (or even triple-track) in parallel careers (not hobbies).
e. Keep on doing what I'm doing, even past retirement age.

10. What do I want for my children?

The purpose of halftime is to take stock, to listen, and to learn. The cry of the psalmist resonates within the hearts of all who grow weary of the first half: "Search me, God, and know my heart; test me and know my anxious thoughts. See if there is any offensive way in me, and lead me in the way everlasting" (Psalm 139:23–24).

CHAPTER 8

What Do You Believe?

I do not recall ever *not* believing in God, and I have a hunch (bolstered by many popular opinion polls) that most Americans also share this view. But for some reason, most of us seem stuck somewhere between disbelief and the quiet confidence that comes from knowing God. Why is that? Why did I spend so much of my first half trying to nail down what God was really like?

Part of this struggle with belief is a good thing. After all, God is at once simple and complex. The concept of an all-knowing, all-powerful, and personal Almighty is a pretty big package to wrap your arms around. The struggle with belief also comes from the very nature of who and what we are during the first half. In our best "conquering" mode, just as we chase the big deal or measure success by the size of our income, we may be unknowingly trying to add God to our list of achievements or to quantify him. We study, analyze, dissect, and fathom until we can say, with great certainty and not a small measure of pride, that we have *acquired* God.

Here is where I believe the church has not been very helpful, for it seems to assume that those of us who sit in the pews and place our offering in the passing plates do not really believe. But the millions who go to church Sunday after Sunday do so, for the most part, because they *do* believe in God. They are not atheists or pagan reprobates. They are God-seeking, if not God-fearing people who, unlike their secular counterparts, got up on a day off, got dressed up, and went to church. And most of them, once they get there, usually sit for an hour or more listening to a minister tell them things they already believe.

This can't go on forever. You can only hear so many sermons, attend so many Bible studies, and spend so much time looking inward. Halftime is the perfect opportunity to shift from trying to *understand* God to learning to *know* him. It is the time to humbly accept the fact that you may never fully understand him, but that you need to accept, by faith, that you are known and loved by him.

The late Jim Russell was a Michigan businessman who, after starting a business from the ground up and working hard to turn it into a very successful enterprise, began investing the lion's share of his time and energy into true second-half kingdom-building work. As a way to get more Christians to do something with their belief in God, Jim established the Amy Awards writing contest. The contest is simple: cash prizes ($10,000 to first place) are awarded to writers of articles that quote the Bible and support Christian teaching in secular newspapers or magazines.

Jim's goal was to encourage Christians to come out of hiding and take their rightful place in a diverse culture. His theory was that the proclamation victory has already been won — that is, the vast majority of Americans have heard the gospel and have responded favorably, but they just don't know what to do about their beliefs. He believed that once Christians learn what to do about what they believe, they can transform our nation. Pretty radical stuff from a conservative businessman, but his point is worth noting.

Sometimes I think we have complicated one of the simplest truths of the Bible: believe on the Lord Jesus Christ and you will be saved. These wonderful words of comfort do not necessarily mean that belonging to a church, having perfect insight into Christian theology, espousing the "right" position on church controversies, or giving to the correct charities will put you in a right relationship with Jesus. These things are not unimportant, but it may be time to ask yourself whether you are worrying too much about them. Then ask yourself, *Is this what I want to be doing for the rest of my life? Is this what faith in Christ ought to be all about?*

According to God's Word, becoming a Christian is an act of acceptance and belief. Accept Jesus as the Son of God and believe that he alone can save you from sin, and you are standing on first base. You do not need to wrestle with belief, because it is settled.

Do you believe? And do you believe so simply, with such childlike faith, that you are ready to put God completely in the box? Are you ready to get on with the second half of your life by moving beyond belief into action?

When I went to Mike Kami, I believed I was a Christian. After all, I had been given the gift of faith at an early age. But like many of those in the first half, my faith was very personal — something that was not quite ready to be shared. This insightful atheist forced me to settle the issue of belief in a dramatic and life-changing way by asking me to identify what was most important to me.

I have a friend who is a brilliant businessman — the kind of guy most would say has it made. He built a publishing empire around a simple idea and in the process has acquired all the accoutrements of success. In addition, he has a lovely wife and a picture-book family, and he is an active church member. Trim and fit and barely forty, he could retire tomorrow and enjoy the fruits of his success for the rest of his life. Instead, he is facing the real possibility of his wife leaving him. I know the situation well enough to be certain there is no "other man" in her life and that he has been faithful to her. I also believe they love each other very much. But they are about to join the ranks of similar American family tragedies because my friend cannot bring himself to place just one thing in the box. In typical first-half fashion, he wants to have it all and is destroying himself and his family by trying to keep all the balls in the air.

You can keep the box empty only for so long. If you do not choose the one thing that belongs in the box, life's inertia will choose it for you. If my friend does not make a deliberate choice on his own, his business will force its way into the box. My guess is that most of the divorces that occur within the church are the result of letting something else decide what's in the box — letting circumstances settle the issue of how your belief is going to affect your commitments.

Do you see why it is important to settle this issue? In the first half, too many things were leading you away from the most important question in your life. You are in halftime because you do not want to go on any longer without finding the answer. The still, small voice has finally gotten your attention, and you know you cannot return to the playing field without responding.

It's a question you *must* answer if you want your second half to be different — and better — than the first half of your life: What's in *your* box?

CHAPTER 9

Finding Your One Thing

Here is a parable from the Wild West as scripted by Holly-wood. It is taken from what I consider to be the central scene in the movie *City Slickers*, starring Billy Crystal and the late Jack Palance.

Let me set the stage. The characters played by Palance and Crystal are riding slowly across the range on horseback, discuss-ing life and love. Palance plays a wily cowpoke, while Crystal is a tenderfoot from Los Angeles who has paid for a two-week dude ranch vacation. Of course, he gets more than he bargained for, and in the process, Crystal learns something important about himself.

Listen carefully to their slightly edited conversation:

CRYSTAL: ... and the second it's over, she's going to get back into her spaceship and fly away for eternity. Would you do it?

PALANCE: She a redhead?

CRYSTAL: Could be.

PALANCE: I like redheads.

CRYSTAL: You ever been married?

PALANCE: Nah.

CRYSTAL: You ever been in love?

PALANCE: Once. I was driving a herd across the panhandle — Texas. Passed through this little dirt farm right about sundown. Out in the field was this young woman working down in the dirt. Just about then, she stood up and stretched her back. She was wearing a little cotton dress, and the settin' sun was right behind her showin' the shape that God had given her.

CRYSTAL: What happened?

PALANCE: I just turned around and rode away.

CRYSTAL: Why?

PALANCE: I figured it wasn't going to get any better than that.

CRYSTAL: Yeah, but you could have been, you know, with her.

PALANCE: I've been with lots of women.

CRYSTAL: Yeah, but, you know, she could have been the love of your life.

PALANCE: She is.

CRYSTAL: That's great. That's ... not great. No, that's wrong, Curly. You passed up something that might have been terrific.

PALANCE: My choice.

CRYSTAL: I never could have done that.

PALANCE: That's your choice. Cowboy leads a different kind of life. When there *were* cowboys. They're a dying breed. Still means something to me, though. In a couple of days, we'll move this herd across the river, drive them through the valley. Ahhh, (*chuckles*) there's nothing like bringing in the herd.

CRYSTAL: You see, now, that's great. Your life makes sense to you.

PALANCE: (*Laughs*)

CRYSTAL: What? What's so funny?

PALANCE: You city folk. You worry about a lot of s——, don't you?

CRYSTAL: S——? My wife basically told me she doesn't want me around.

PALANCE: She a redhead?

CRYSTAL: I'm just saying ...

PALANCE: How old are you? Thirty-eight?

CRYSTAL: Thirty-nine.

PALANCE: Yeah. You all come out here about the same age. Same problems. Spend fifty weeks a year getting knots in your rope then ... then you think two weeks up here will untie them for you. None of you get it. (*Long pause*) Do you know what the secret of life is?

CRYSTAL: No, what?

PALANCE: This. (*Holds up his index finger*)

CRYSTAL: Your finger?

PALANCE: One thing. Just one thing. You stick to that and everything else don't mean s——.

CRYSTAL: That's great, but what's the one thing?

PALANCE: That's what you've got to figure out.[1]

When I first saw that scene, I recognized it immediately as a parable that uncovers a deep truth. It speaks to persons in the first half with particular resonance and rings with authenticity and wisdom. Jack Palance, the weather-beaten, wizened old philosopher with a Stetson pulled low on his forehead and a cigarette dangling from his lips, speaks the spare and sage words that are true for you and me. They are not especially elegant words, but they are eloquent in communicating a powerful message.

Palance's sentiment is remarkably similar to one voiced by Eric Hoffer, the American longshoreman philosopher who shrewdly observed that "the feeling of being hurried is not usually the result of living a full life and having no time. It is, on the contrary, born of a vague fear that we are wasting our life. When we do not do the one thing we ought to do, we have no time for anything else — we are the busiest people in the world."[2] In the first half of your life, you may have often felt you were one of the busiest people in the world. The key to a successful second half is finding your "one thing" and, in the process, finding what the Bible calls a state of joy, or blessedness.

Most people never discover their "one thing." But part of

what is so unsettling about approaching the end of the first half of our lives is that we know it is out there somewhere. Like Billy Crystal's character, we desperately long to find it, but we don't know for sure where to look. Too often we try to fill that void with things that offer only temporary relief, such as making and spending money, getting involved in projects and competition (winning), and forming relationships.

Larry Crabb, author of *Inside Out*, refers to this longing as a desire to fill a "hollow place located centrally within us ... the core desire of our soul."[3] The seventeenth-century French philosopher Blaise Pascal called it the "God-shaped vacuum." As you first began to experience success in your career, you satisfied this core desire by accumulating and achieving — remember, the first half is the hunter-gatherer mode. The proof is in your attic, garage, and closets! Note also how much time you devote to recreation, leisure, and social activities.

Are all of these activities bad? Of course you know they aren't, but they will never satisfy that longing to find the "one thing" that is uniquely yours — the thing that, once found, will enable you to make a difference.

God has programmed your "one thing" into your life like computer software. The apostle Paul writes about this in his epistle to the church at Ephesus: "For we are God's handiwork, created in Christ Jesus to do good works, which God prepared in advance for us to do" (Ephesians 2:10). Your one thing is the most essential part of you, your transcendent dimension. It is discovering what's true about yourself, rather than overlaying someone else's truth on you or injecting someone else's goals into your personality.

Figuring out what's in the box will settle the issue of who or what will be the foundation of your life. It also will settle the belief issue. But it's not enough just to identify what's in the box; you must also know who is holding it, who you are as a unique individual created for a purpose by God. What is your purpose? What makes you tick? What do you do so well that you would enjoy doing it without pay? What is your passion, the spark that needs only a little breeze to ignite into a raging fire?

We do not ask those questions during the first half of our lives because we are too busy doing what we think is right. But if it is beginning to seem as if the "right thing" is not your "one thing," you have reached the closing seconds of your first half. This is what Peter Drucker meant when he explained the difference between efficiency and effectiveness. Efficiency, Peter said, is doing things right. Effectiveness is doing the right things.

I would like to be more helpful than Jack Palance was for Billy Crystal, but finding your one thing really is your task. All I can tell you with any degree of certainty is that you will not find an abiding sense of purpose and direction by rushing from business appointment to church meeting to your child's soccer game to dinner with friends and then to bed. If you cannot afford to spend the time in solitude with God that finding your "one thing" requires, you are not ready to find it.

CHAPTER 10

From Success to Significance

There are two sources of unhappiness in life.
One is not getting what you want; the other is getting it.
George Bernard Shaw

Why would former Philadelphia mayor Wilson Goode, after leaving office, go from church to church recruiting mentors for at-risk teenagers and children of prisoners? Why would Michael Jordan leave a game in which he was the dominant player on a world championship team and settle for a minor league spot on a second-rate team in another sport?

Why would Tom Tierney leave a seven-figure job as CEO of world-class Bain & Companies to form Bridgespan, which focuses exclusively on midlevel nonprofit organizations? And why are you clicking on websites like *monster.com* and *Career-Builder.com*, looking at a possible career change, dreaming about owning a little restaurant, or maybe considering a short-term missions assignment?

One of the most common characteristics of a person who is nearing the end of the first half is that unquenchable desire to move from success to significance. After a first half of building a career and trying to become financially secure, we'd like to do something in the second half that is more meaningful — something that rises above perks and paychecks into the stratosphere of significance.

Not that success is all bad. America is crazy about success, and for good reasons. From the earliest days of our youth we are encouraged to compete for the top prize, whether the contest is schoolyard tag or a classroom spelling bee. (I still, to this day, remember winning the first-grade spelling bee in Okmulgee, Oklahoma.) High school students study to achieve the highest possible ranking in their graduating class so that they will gain acceptance to the top universities, which then put them on the right path toward a prized position in a prestigious firm. In turn, employers who gather enough of these front-runners hope to see their company's name at the top of somebody's "best of" list in a leading publication.

I have been in business all my life and have yet to run into a company that deliberately tried to become second best. Nor should they. The drive to become the best is a powerful and positive motivator — it is the engine that drives not only a vibrant economy but a whole way of life that treats excellence as though it is attainable. And even when we fall short of the prize, the effort has lifted us above our expectations.

The good life, in the most positive use of that term, is the result of a healthy desire to be successful. But on our way to becoming successful, we begin to pick up signals that tell us success isn't enough. You may be reading some of these signals:

The thrill of closing a major deal isn't quite what it was ten years ago.

Younger associates are nipping at your heels, and you respond by offering to mentor them rather than trying to stay ahead of them.

You spend a lot of time thinking what it might be like to start over or move "down" to a less responsible position that gives you more control of your life.

You have a secure position, yet you're frequently surfing the Internet for other jobs or career possibilities.

You wonder more about what makes clients tick than how to sell them on a proposal.

You envy those who walk away from their jobs to spend more time with their families and the ministry work they've been dreaming about.

You use up all your vacation days and start taking some "comp time" as well.

You begin to ask yourself, "How much is enough?"

The boss's hint of a promotion doesn't motivate you as much as it used to.

You've been thinking very seriously about starting your own business.

Your teenager says to you one day, "Get a life."

Psychologist Donald Joy once observed that soon after a man turns forty, he is likely to tackle a huge undertaking — something that appears to be slightly out of his reach. If he's a farmer, he takes out a loan and expands the farm so that it is the biggest in the county. If he's a midlevel manager in an established company, he leaves to form his own business. Or he may try to make his mark in his hobby or avocation. A recreational rock climber, for example, may attempt to climb a major peak, or a Saturday sailor may try a solo ocean cruise.

Some may consider this ambitious push to excel yet another attempt to be successful, but it's more than that. As we move closer to the halftime of our lives, we realize that we can only buy, sell, manage, and attain so much. We also begin to understand that we will *live* only so long. When all is said and done, our success will be pretty empty unless it has included a corresponding degree of significance — and much of what we do in the first half is not imbued with the presence of the eternal. As one successful Harvard-educated businessman remarked about the many successes he had experienced in his business, "I was always finding out that beyond the pot of gold at the end of the rainbow, there's a sort of emptiness."

Consider my friend Howard. Several years ago he was in his midforties and served as chairman, president, and CEO of his firm, which was the largest of its type in the city where he lived. He was also the most driven and compulsive person in an organization of high-powered, ambitious people called the Young Presidents Organization (YPO), to which I also belonged.

The trade press that covers his industry has called Howard the "Great White Shark" and has compared him to "a heat-seeking missile," descriptions intended — and taken — as compliments. The division Howard oversaw was the crown jewel in a very large service industry holding company, and there was wide speculation that someday he would be asked to move to New York City to take the top job in the corporation.

Howard was a super success. I had dinner with him at a YPO meeting several years ago, and he told me what accounted for his success.

"My career is what matters," he said. "I do four client dinners a week. I'm not home much, but my family has to understand that the job comes first. We get quality time on vacation, but that's about it for the year. That's just the way it is."

Then a rogue wave took a run at Howard: he lost his only son in an accident.

There was nothing in Howard that prepared him for the loss of his son — absolutely nothing. He was grief-stricken and tormented by all manner of unanswerable questions. After the accident, when I saw Howard at YPO meetings, he would say quietly to me, "I'm not handling this very well. We've got to talk." Yet he didn't call. He poured himself even more single-mindedly into his work. But I could see in his eyes that something had snapped; his work wasn't working for him anymore.

A few months later, I once again sat next to Howard at a YPO function. He leaned close and told me that he was staying on until the end of the year, but that his resignation and announcement of his handpicked successor would appear in the next day's newspaper. He wasn't sure what he would be doing after that, but the thrill of the chase in business had absolutely lost its attraction for him as the full-time organizing principle of his life.

Then, with a broadening grin on his face, Howard informed me that he had spent the previous week calling his largest clients to inform them of his departure. "Something really strange happened during those calls," he said. "These guys are just like me, guys my age, hard drivers, tough, ambitious. I got virtually the identical reaction from each of them. First of all, I was greeted by about twenty seconds of pure silence, and then the guy would say, 'You son of a gun. You beat me to it. My wife and I have been talking about doing the same thing.'"

The last time I called Howard's office, he had skipped out to play basketball with inner-city kids at a recreation center. It was 10:00 a.m. on a weekday. His secretary said he would get back to me, but I told her there was no rush.

Howard had passed from the first half into halftime right before my eyes. He was discovering what was in the box. Unfortunately, it took a tragedy to get his attention.

Success often involves carrying your box with you as you head for the top but never knowing what's in it. Significance begins by stopping wherever you are in the journey to see what's in the box and then reordering your life around its contents. For the Christian, this may mean putting God in the box and then following wherever that decision leads. Unfortunately, most think successful Christians in business are just rich people who give a lot of money to the church. Significance comes when those businesspeople find a way to give *themselves* to God (if, indeed, God is in the box). That may or may not require a change of jobs, but it always requires a change of attitude. Dennis O'Connor and Donald M. Wolfe, in the *Journal of Organizational Behavior*, call this change in attitude a "personal paradigm shift (i.e., major changes in one's system of perceptions, beliefs, values, and feelings)."[1] I sometimes call it a reordering of our personal myth.

For me it meant handing over the day-to-day operation of my business to others so that I could be free to work directly with church leaders. That was my calling, the way I felt God was leading me to serve him. Before, I tithed from a substantial income and occasionally added to it with personal gifts; now I give approximately 75 percent of myself to causes that match up to the way God wired me.

You see, I don't believe that God creates us with specialized abilities and temperaments and then asks us to do things for him that require completely different abilities and temperaments. Why would a Creator who put together such an efficient and sensible natural world violate his design template when it came to humans?

I recall an acquaintance who had a brilliant track record as a systems analyst. He was approaching halftime and wondered if there might be a way to devote more of his time and talent to God. The well-meaning pastor of his church "challenged" him to volunteer to teach a junior high Sunday school class! Nothing against teaching Sunday school (I've been doing it for years), but this guy could have been a valuable resource to the church through his computer and business skills. What he wanted was to move from success to significance, but he was offered a chance at almost certain failure. Which would you choose?

Significance need not be a 180-degree course change. Instead, do some retrofitting so that you can apply your gifts in ways that allow you to spend more time on things related to what's in your box. And do it in such a way as to reclaim the thrill of that first deal! God has a wonderful plan for the second half of your life: to allow you to serve him by doing what you like to do and what you are good at.

CHAPTER 11

Finding the Center and Staying There

At the still point of the turning world.... There the dance is. Where the past and future are gathered.... The inner freedom from practical desire, the release from action and suffering. Release from inner and outer compulsion.

An adaptation of "Four Quartets" by T. S. Eliot
— in calligraphy on the wall at Still Point Farm

I have always been drawn toward the center. Even in my first half — a time when most of us tend to flit frenetically between the anxiety of the chase and the boredom between deals — I was always able to somehow find my way back to the middle. I think I am just wired that way.

If my "centeredness" was a matter of luck in my first half, however, it is now a conscious choice. You can be lucky only so long. One of the warning signals of the end of the first half is the sense that you shouldn't spend too much time at either extreme. It is important to be deliberate about finding and holding in comfortable balance the creative tension that is the reality of life. Halftime gives us a chance to pause and identify the extremes between which we are caught and then to determine how to live peacefully with them in the second half.

It can be done.

Harvard ethicist Laura Nash's instructive book *Believers in*

Business is filled with stories of Christians living in the real world of the marketplace. In her research for the book, Nash conducted a study of sixty evangelical chief executive officers to discover how they balanced the competing tensions of their work.

First, consider the seven tensions she identified as common to Christians in the marketplace:

serving God vs. pursuing mammon

love vs. competition

people needs vs. profit obligations

family vs. work

keeping personal perspective in the face of success

charity vs. wealth

being a faithful witness in a pluralistic workplace[1]

Sound familiar? Do you ever feel caught between any of these extremes? If you view these tensions negatively, you are probably still in the first half. But when you begin to see that these tensions are not only necessary but may have some benefits, you have entered halftime. In your journey into the second half, you will find ways to reduce the tension by learning how to deal with paradox. In other words, you will find peace in knowing that you will never resolve the tension — it will always be there, and there is nothing inherently wrong with it.

It sounds almost simplistic to report that Dr. Nash identifies two key words that describe how those sixty Christian CEOs positively handled these tensions: *balance* and *faith*. If this sounds familiar, it is probably because the Bible has taught clearly that life is seldom an either/or proposition — that paradox is not bad. We learn this in the familiar words of Ecclesiastes 3:

There is a time for everything,
and a season for every activity under the heavens:

a time to be born and a time to die,
a time to plant and a time to uproot ...
a time to mourn and a time to dance ... (vv. 1–4)

And later:

I have seen the burden God has laid on the human race. He has made everything beautiful in its time. (vv. 10–11)

Paul, too, speaks clearly of the "both/and" nature of life:

Rather, as servants of God we commend ourselves in every way: in great endurance; in troubles, hardships and distresses; in beatings, imprisonments and riots; in hard work, sleepless nights and hunger; in purity, understanding, patience and kindness; in the Holy Spirit and in sincere love; in truthful speech and in the power of God; with weapons of righteousness in the right hand and in the left; through glory and dishonor, bad report and good report; genuine, yet regarded as impostors; known, yet regarded as unknown; dying, and yet we live on; beaten, and yet not killed; sorrowful, yet always rejoicing; poor, yet making many rich; having nothing, and yet possessing everything. (2 Corinthians 6:4–10)

That pretty much covers the waterfront, doesn't it? It was no different for any of the major Bible heroes — for Abraham or Joseph or Moses or David or the apostles — so who are *we* to expect comfortable, predictable lives? Instead, we are called to live somewhere in the middle of the tension and the paradox. And not just to exist in some spirit of tolerance, but actually to thrive! In athletics it is called the "zone" — that moment in time and space when the tensions of winning and losing, physics and the supernatural, man and spirit, are suspended ever so briefly for one game, one play, one hit.

Unfortunately, organized religion emphasizes a coming apart from chaos and confusion. (One pastor I know refers to the pulpit as being "ten feet safely above contradiction.") As far back as the Middle Ages, monasticism and religious orders have viewed religious life as a haven from the sin and hurly-burly of the streets. And today we still view a serious religious life as something separate from the rest of the world — a career for credentialed professionals only.

In reality — a reality the world needs to see — Christ meets us and works with us in the confusion, in the valley of the shadow of death, in the tunnel of chaos when the familiar landmarks have disappeared. And he is there with me on a ridge above the Rio Grande River, as I beat on the steering wheel of a rental car, wailing in grief over the loss of my son, tears and nosebleed raining down on my sweater, screaming out in pain at the horror of my loss.

He is there with me.

Most people who are in their first half want their lives orderly and neat, their religion rational. In reality, however, we are suspended between the extremes of order and confusion, the known and the unknown. And only when we begin to settle our first-half issues and relinquish control over that desire to order our own lives will we be able to live comfortably in tension.

In my own pilgrimage, I have come to refer to this position of balance as the "J-Zone." On the extremes are anxiety and boredom. Neither is comfortable, nor is a life that finds us moving out of one and into the other and back again over and over and over. Yet that is how most of us live in the first half.

It was only after I named what was in my box that I began to learn how to live comfortably with both anxiety and boredom. The closer I stayed to my center — Jesus — the more accepting I became of paradox. Anxiety and boredom were still there, but now I could keep them at bay. I could be chasing down a major deal one day and reading Chaucer the next and somehow see how the in-between transcended both. In the J-Zone, I found that work and family are not either/or, that faith and the market do not exclude one another, that winning and losing are both okay.

Please do not mistake balance — the J-Zone — for success. To suggest that placing Jesus Christ at the center of my life resulted in overwhelming success would be dishonest and misleading. It has, however, quenched for me, as it will for you, the thirst for success by pouring the more satisfying draught of significance into my cup.

Let me give you an example. Soon after I met with Mike Kami and answered the question, "What's in the box?" I was confronted with a tremendous business opportunity. It was a delicious-looking deal with a staggering potential payoff. As I pondered whether to jump in, I happened to be on an airplane bound for Washington, D.C., and seated across the aisle from me was the head of a major federal agency, a man whose bureau would have a good deal to do with the very investment I was contemplating. As it happened, I knew him personally; he had been my lawyer before going to Washington.

I explained to him the opportunity and told him about my competing desire to serve Christ through my gift of entrepreneurship by allocating the majority of my time to a life of service. And then I asked him what he would do if he were in my shoes. Without hesitating, he said, "It seems to me you are standing on a mountaintop, and this is your temptation."

I asked this man if he was a student of the Bible, and he replied, "Not really." But I knew that somewhere, somehow, he had drawn on a truth from the Bible. The first thing I did when I got to my hotel room was to search through the bedside Gideon Bible. Sure enough, what my friend was referring to was the second of the three temptations Satan put before Christ in the book of Matthew — the temptation for Jesus to do something spectacular, something that defied all the laws of gravity, something that proved that God had such special regard for him that he could defy natural law. The tempter's voice says, "Go for it! This is your chance! Throw all your inhibition and caution to the wind! You'll never see this opportunity again."

The deal I was looking at defied several of the business world's laws of gravity. Although the return would be spectacular if it played out, it was a tax-driven venture in a business I knew nothing about. My inner voice said, "Life really isn't that easy. Stick to the things you know. Play out of the knowledge your experience has entitled you to possess."

Once again, someone who was not a particularly zealous Christian had led me to the deep truth that Scripture has for all of us. I became more convinced than ever that God uses all kinds of people to get us the help we need if we will just be aware and sensitive. The man had seen clearly what I was perceiving only dimly. My conversation with him helped steer me back to my core, to my central values, from which I was tempted to stray. When I got back from Washington, I placed a phone call: the deal would have to be done without me.

In my first half, I would have considered that a deal I had lost. In my second, I accept it not as a win or a loss, but as one of those transcendent experiences in which I know and am comfortable with who I am and what I am here for.

If you find yourself yearning to respond similarly to a loss, maybe you are getting ready for *your* second half.

CHAPTER 12

Staying in the Game
but Adjusting the Plan

My second half began when I walked away from my full-time, hands-on involvement with my business. You probably can't do that. But even if you can't, you can still have a significant second half.

By the time you get into halftime, your attitude toward your job may range from "I love my job so much I'd do it even if they didn't pay me" to "I can't stand what I do no matter how much money I make." I was fortunate enough to be pretty close to the first response, but I realize there are many who are closer to the second. In fact, my hunch is that quite a few people do not like their jobs very much and use them mainly as a means to an end.

I recall a young man who was a cold call, straight commission salesperson. He was one of those guys who didn't make a penny if he didn't sell something. No base salary. No drawing a salary on his commission. Just knock on doors and try to sell, and in this case, he sold fairly low-ticket items: notions and knick-knacks to general stores and hardware stores.

But this guy was good: he sold enough to earn a six-figure income. That's a ton of knickknacks! Like most salespeople, he had a lot of drive and a lot of enthusiasm. In fact, he was so enthusiastic that I remarked about how much he must love selling. "I hate it," he replied. "But I love the pay." I mused to myself, recalling how my son, Ross, used to say, "I want to live to work, not work to live."

For me my career demanded just those things I enjoyed giving, and it rewarded me with a great deal of satisfaction and with not a little money. To me, there was nothing more exhilarating than putting together a deal, negotiating the details, then celebrating after the handshake. I loved to develop a strategy to make the deal work. I was successful and received plenty of strokes, so it was not easy for me to decide to hand over the day-to-day operation of my business to a team of other people. In a sense, I was depriving myself of the pleasure I derived from my job.

Some people think that their problems would be over if they could just walk away from their jobs as I was able to do. To be truthful, a successful halftime experience shouldn't begin with the fact that you hate your job. One of the things I've learned as I've watched and helped people transition into their second half is that halftime is not an escape or a more respectable midlife crisis. It really shouldn't be a reaction to something negative in your life as much as a response to positive hopes and ambitions you are feeling. One of the reasons why so many people stay in the first half is that their focus is on the rat race rather than on their contributions, talents, and calling; so instead of planning a successful midlife transition that would allow them to do more of what they love, they jump ship. Change jobs. Start a business. Go independent.

None of the above are bad options, but I plead with you: beware of the urge to "get away from it all." That is not what the second half is all about. I know people who are well into their second halves who are still working at the same job they started with and who will be there to get the gold watch. The key to a successful second half is not a change of jobs; it is a change of heart, a change in the way you view the world and order your life. That might involve a completely new career or holding on to your present position. Usually it is something between the two.

Seismic Testing

Being from Texas, I can't help but have learned a few things about the oil business. I'm far from being an expert, mind you, but one of the things I have learned is that you don't just go out and pick a spot and start drilling. If you want to minimize your risks, you do some seismic testing — which is basically a sophisticated way to check out the landscape to see what it might produce. Since the size and shape of a subsurface formation is unknown, an electronic device is used to shoot sonarlike impulses down toward the formation from different points of view. The matter starts to take shape as it is seen from the various perspectives.

In terms of second-half seismic testing, your "subsurface formation" is that imponderable matter regarding how you will restructure your life. Your idea is indistinct in size and shape, and you can see it only from a limited viewpoint, so you go to six or eight different people you trust and ask them how *they* see it. Their "sonar" will reflect a part of the picture that you could not see before, and eventually the most inchoate and vaguest matters will begin to assume a definite size and shape. Then at least you know whether to drill or not.

You may think that once I decided what was in the box, I quickly handed the reins of my business over to a subordinate and walked out the door looking for new, albeit tamer, dragons to slay. Believe me, that would have been a big mistake, even though I was financially set for life and could afford some false starts. Instead, I did some seismic testing. I knew that I was gifted in the area of human organizations, and I also knew I enjoyed working in that area immensely. I could have stayed on in the human organization I had built, for I was assured continued success there, but I had already tasted success; it was significance I was after — something that got closer to both who I was and what was in the box. I did not see my cable television business as a primary source of significance in my life.

Neither did my adviser, Mike Kami. His advice was simple, and I wasn't quite ready for it: "Sell your company and invest the money in the ministry-oriented projects you've been talking about."

I sat there, stunned by the implications of this decision. Linda appeared no less stunned. I could almost see the stereotypical images of ministers, missionaries, and monastics passing through her mind. Would we be a philanthropic couple passing out money until our sack was empty? Would we be required to dress differently like so many professional religious people and their spouses do? Had life as we'd known and enjoyed it come to a sudden, crashing, newly impoverished end?

Fortunately, I did some seismic testing. I sought the advice of two Christian leaders: Ray Stedman, then pastor of a church in Palo Alto, California, and James Dobson, popular author and founder of Focus on the Family. Each in his own way warned me: "If you sell your company, you will lose your platform and no one will return your calls." It was clear that I needed to be far more certain about where I was going with my life before I made any big plans.

So I called together a group of trusted advisers that included Fred Smith Sr., Paul Robbins, and Harold Myra of *Christianity Today*. Together they had a broad overview and deep knowledge of the area in which I was preparing to work: the body of Christ in the United States. They knew how much I enjoyed working on organizational schemes and that I wanted to spend a good share of my time on kingdom work. I asked them, "What are the opportunities for someone with my particular design?"

They reminded me of a new breed of churches that was very

large and attempting to do church differently. "Maybe you could help them somehow," they suggested. So I invited a group of pastors together, asked Paul to serve as a nondirective moderator to ask them some questions, then sat back and listened.

Listening is a big part of seismic testing; it helps you discover areas of usefulness. I learned what these pastors perceived would be useful to them and then continued my testing by facilitating focus groups of senior pastors from large churches. Eventually these pastors narrowed down their discussions to three things they felt would be useful to them, and I saw my second-half calling take shape.

As a direct result of this kind of testing, I was able to develop a network and support system that serves a unique group of people in Christian ministry. There is nothing magic about pastors of large churches; it just happens that, in God's providence, my interest in human organizations matched up nicely with their need to understand the dynamics of what is happening with their churches. If I was wired differently, I could have been hooked up just as easily with executives of overseas missions agencies or a network of small, rural churches. But had I rushed out of my session with Mike Kami and jumped at the first church-type job available, I probably would not have found something so closely aligned to who I am.

There are two keys to successful seismic testing. The first is to know who you are, and the second is to seek out reliable counsel. When I sought guidance from two friends, I asked, "What can I do to be useful?" They responded, "What does the 'I' consist of?" In other words, who am I? That's a very important question for anyone looking into the second half, because you cannot operate out of a strength that God doesn't give you.

Suppose you have often felt guilty about not doing enough evangelizing, so when your second half rolls around, you decide to quit your job to become a preacher or a missionary. Instead, it might be much better to begin this decision-making process with a full knowledge and acceptance of who you are. Honestly assess your gifts and abilities. Is evangelism your gift? If it is something you enjoy doing and can do well, then do some seismic testing before you sign up for seminary or head to Africa. Assist your pastor on some calls to people interested in learning about Jesus or volunteer for a short-term missions assignment. If these brief explorations come back positive, then get more serious about what to do. If they come back negative, you will have saved yourself a lot of trouble.

What you do best for God will rise out of that core being he has created within you. Do you remember our Lord's parable of the talents? The wonderful message from this story is that you and I will be held accountable only for what we were given, not for what others might have or expect from us. In Jesus' parable, the guy who was given only two talents and doubled them was esteemed as highly as the guy who started out with five. We are not all given the same equipment, but we are expected to know what we were given and find ways to invest ourselves wisely.

Low-Cost Probes

I have a friend almost exactly my age who had come to a point similar to my own at halftime. He decided that God was the central motivating factor in his life and that he wanted to find some way of giving his gift of leadership back to God. At about the same time, he was offered the CEO spot in a two-billion-dollar, highly leveraged company with operations ranging as far west as Thailand and as far east as Europe. It would be a tough, demanding, and challenging job with plenty of prestige and an annual salary approaching a million dollars. It was the type of position that people in the business community would die for — in fact, many do.

But if he took the job, he would be committed to at least five years — time that he had hoped to be spending in kingdom work.

He had also been thinking about going to seminary, so he came to me with these two choices: Fortune 500 or Hermeneutics 101. He had already made the decision to put God in the box, but he did not know whether that meant full-time, professional Christian ministry or something else.

I told him to take the CEO spot, forget about seminary, and engage in some low-cost probes. To me, he had no choice. If he went to seminary, he would emerge three years later as a rank amateur at over fifty years of age. He might land an associate minister's job at a larger church and, by the time he was fifty-five, get a senior position at a church struggling to keep its head above water. Did my friend really think God gave him twenty-five years of training in business management and executive leadership so that he could pastor a medium-sized church struggling to find itself?

That did not mean, however, that my friend needed to disavow his allegiance to God. Low-cost probes involve practical explorations in the field or fields in which you think you would like to spend your second half. My friend, for example, may need to stay in the midst of international business but look into starting an informal network of Bible studies for other CEOs. It would take some phone calls, some emails, and a couple of trial balloons to show him if that is really a need and if he's the one to fill it. Or, if he senses the need to eventually leave his career and work more in professional ministry, he might consider doing some consulting for Christian organizations — pro bono, if necessary.

My inviting a group of pastors to a meeting is another example of a low-cost probe. I had done my seismic testing by seeking out the counsel of trusted advisers who pointed me in the right direction, but I did not jump in with both feet. If that first meeting of pastors had fallen flat, my investment of time and money was such that I could have easily tried something else.

The point of low-cost probes is to gain some hands-on experience in combining your gifts with service to God and the church. It's done in business all the time in the form of market research, product testing, pilot projects, and the like. The reason people don't do it individually as they approach the second half is that they are still doing things the first-half way: full speed ahead with both feet. Remember, this second-half decision is about something more important than just another investment, just another sale. Slow down. Be deliberate. Test the waters.

The Half-Speed Option

Let's say you really like your job, and frankly, you feel you need it. You need the security of a regular paycheck, health insurance, and pension, and you also enjoy the identity it gives you. You like being sales manager for Midtown Associates. Can someone like you look forward to a rewarding second half?

Actually, many people fit this description. And the group really grows when we add those who don't necessarily like their work but who find that leaving is not an option. The good news is that people in this group certainly can have a second half that is better than the first. Let's face it. By the time you've been at something for ten to twenty years, you've pretty well mastered it. You've learned to delegate, you have a network of people you know, you are familiar with the landscape, you've grown a productive list of clients, and you've found ways to get through each day without rushing at breakneck speed.

If you're really honest with yourself, you can probably work at half speed and still excel. That's what a lawyer friend of mine is doing. He is a senior partner in a very prestigious law firm that handles cases for some of the most powerful and famous people in the country. Scott (not his real name) loved what he was doing and was world class at it, yet he sensed there was more to life than putting together megadeals — he sensed that he was missing something. There were second-half things he wanted to do, but he didn't want to walk away from a practice he had worked so hard to build. Then he realized he could stay with his firm and still have time to invest himself in a very worthy project involving the public school systems around his state. Now when you ask him what he does for a living, he responds, somewhat facetiously, "I'm trying to convince my law partners that I still practice law." What he's really doing is taking half the time it used to take to drive his career and putting it into this new second-half commitment.

Or consider another acquaintance who is a public school teacher. He's one of the best science teachers in his state and would just as soon retire "in the saddle," but he too has some second-half goals to pursue. One of these is to use his administrative skills to provide business leadership for his local church. He started out just like my lawyer friend: hard charging, working sixteen-hour days, pushing the envelope to become top in his field. Both men love their work and do not feel it's time to leave it, so they are using the additional time and energy that comes from doing a good job at half speed to fulfill their second-half goals.

You see, when it comes to having a better second half than the first, it doesn't matter whether you're a millionaire CEO, a highly paid lawyer, or a teacher. What's important is that you start off by discovering the way God built you so that you can use your uniquely developed talents for him.

CHAPTER 13

Overlapping Curves

*It is one of the paradoxes of success
that the things and ways which got you there
are seldom those things that keep you there.*
Charles Handy

Everything seems to conspire to keep us where we are. That is why so many people remain stuck in the first half or, at best, flounder in a perpetual halftime. Life seems more comfortable in known, familiar territory, even when we are fairly certain something better awaits us out there.

Take the Israelites, for instance. They were forever talking about the Promised Land, but they couldn't bring themselves to leave the familiar territory of Egypt. Not that Egypt was such a great place, but it was known; it had become home. For too many people today, the first half has become home.

I find it interesting that so many contemporary authors have recognized the stage of uncertainty that immobilizes people approaching midlife. William Bridges calls it the "Neutral Zone." Scott Peck calls it the "Tunnel of Chaos." Janet Hagberg calls it "Stage 4: Power by reflection." Whatever its name, it is a zone that must be traversed to get to the promised land of the second half.

Many people don't make it through this zone, which is characterized by the pain of loss of former certainties and by confusion about what comes next. Graphically, it looks like this:

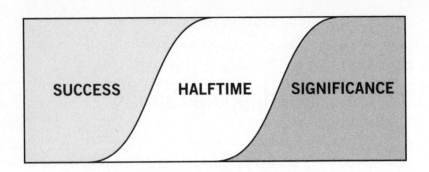

Seeing this time of uncertainty and sensing the pain, risk, and confusion involved in change, we have a tendency to cling to the known. The future seems to be somewhat fuzzy and vague, and it doesn't compete well with the comfort and certainty of our present situation.

Then we can add to that fear of the uncertain these very real questions that haunt us:

"How will I support myself?" (our need for financial security)

"How do you know this new idea will work? It sounds kind of iffy to me." (rational friends)

"What's going on here? This isn't the person I married!" (concerned spouse)

"Exactly what do you do at work?" (worried children)

In his very helpful book *The Age of Paradox*, Charles Handy captures this tension in a chapter titled "The Sigmoid Curve." Handy sets up the problem with the sentence I quoted at the beginning of this chapter and repeat here: "It is one of the paradoxes of success that the things and ways which got you there are seldom those that keep you there."

Handy also offers a solution: "The secret to constant growth is to start a new Sigmoid Curve before the first one peters out. The right place to start that second curve is at Point A (below) where there is the time, as well as the resources and energy, to get the new curve through its initial explorations and flounderings before the first curve begins to dip downward."[1]

THE SIGMOID CURVE
by Charles Handy, *The Age of Paradox*

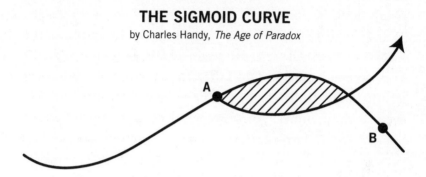

The normal pattern for most people is a single curve that rises as we approach middle age then sharply falls off toward retirement. What Handy recommends is to start a new curve, preferably while the first one is still rising, but certainly before it begins to fall.

Ideally, life should consist of a series of overlapping curves. In my business life, the overlapping curves went something like this:

Before the first curve is played out	Begin the second curve
school	apprentice work
apprentice work	doing work
doing work	leading work
leading work	doing ministry
doing ministry	leading ministry
leading ministry	portfolio of ministries

It is possible to get stuck in any one of these areas. I know people close to my own age who are perpetual students. They acquire degrees like I used to acquire television stations. Others I have known have gotten stuck as the curve of "doing work" began to fall off. Before they knew it, there was no new curve rising on the horizon.

It is important to learn how to enjoy and benefit from the success you worked so hard to attain *without* becoming addicted to it, without going past the inflection point in the curve when it turns sour. Handy's Sigmoid Curve shows us that everything, even the best things, go pathological beyond that inflection point. And it is the realization that they could become stuck forever — "in a rut," as some say — that helps motivate some people to escape the first half.

Part of the key to getting to the second half is the marketing slogan a certain shoe company used to use: "Just do it!" But it is more than that. It is "doing it" at the right time, before your own first curve is picking up speed on the downturn. I know too many people who heard the still, small voice telling them to move on to something better, only to hold the prompting at arm's length. They realized, of course, that the voice was true, but they also knew that to follow it would lead into unfamiliar, uncharted territory. *Better to wait until I am finished with what I am doing*, they thought. But by the time they were finished, it was too late. They were too tired. And the voice was too faint to hear anymore. A well-known strategy consultant for Christian organizations once told me, "I know lots of people who say they are going to invest themselves in Christian work 'someday.' But someday never seems to come. It's just a way of procrastinating. Someday is always never."

Peter Drucker told me that retirees have not proved to be the fertile source of volunteer effort we once thought they would be. They cut their engines off and lose their edge. Peter believed that if you do not have a second or parallel career in service by age forty-five, and if you are not vigorously involved in it by age fifty-five, it will never happen.

If the still, small voice is speaking to you now, do not look for reasons to ignore it. There will always be reasons to stay where you are. It is faith that calls you to move on.

CHAPTER 14

Leaping into the Abyss

We must be doing what we want the world to be.
Mohandas Gandhi

On my desk at home is a plaque that bears a motto of deep importance to me. It says something both serious and playful — serious because of its face-value meaning, yet playful because it came from the classic movie *The Blues Brothers*. Here is what it says: "On a Mission for God."

In the movie, which starred Dan Ackroyd and the late John Belushi as a pair of crazed brothers — Jake and Elwood Blues — Jake tells his brother he's on a mission from God. Unlike them, I'm on a mission *for* God. But just like them, I'm willing to crash a few cars along the way, and I'm inviting you to come along for the ride of your life.

Up to this point, I have tended to focus on the reasons why planning a better second half will be good for you, for indeed it will. But there is a much better reason to search for ways to harness your gifts to God's kingdom during the second half of your life, and that is for the eternal value. God has always promoted win-win situations for his children. What is good for his kingdom is usually better for us as individuals.

For most of your first half, you may have wanted to keep God in the center of your box, but he kept getting squeezed out. I do not consider that wrong as much as inevitable. The demands of life and the nature of youth together make it very difficult to understand the biblical truth that in order to appreciate the magnitude of your individual significance, you must also understand and accept how small you are. While the first half is all about gaining, which sometimes results in loss, the second half is more about releasing and relinquishing, which usually results in strength. You do not see that clearly when you are twenty-six years old.

I have hesitated, at times, to tell my story. I have been so uniquely blessed that I don't want anyone to conclude that only rich people can have a better second half. Please remember that my second half is going well not because I have money, but because I swallowed hard and put one thing in the box. It was not easy for me to do, nor will it be easy for you either. But *that* is what has made the difference.

People who hear me speak often ask me if there are some people who can never have a better second half. In other words, is it ever too late to have a second half? Is a second half only for the upper middle class and above? Is it only for men? Is it only a Christian thing?

I have thought long and hard about this and have concluded that anyone who has grown weary of his or her life can do something to change it for the better. Anyone. I confess that I do not fully understand the unique issues that women face, but I suspect that both women who choose to stay home and those who work in other venues reach a point at which they ask themselves, "Is this as good as it gets?" My answer is the same, regardless of your gender: "No, better things await you."

I am also certain that those who do not profess faith in Christ may also have a better second half. In fact, much of my reading on this subject is from people who probably are not Christians, or at least their material is not presented in Christian or biblical terms. Yet most agree that success eventually loses its luster and that significance is what we're really after. Secular persons generally find significance in some form of altruism; Christians simply have a biblical framework to define their altruism.

So that leaves us with the question of age. Is it ever too late to move from the first half to the second? What about people in their sixties? Seventies? Eighties? As long as we breathe, it is never too late in life to discover a better way. The existential writer Albert Camus discovered this truth: "In the midst of winter I finally learned that there was in me an invincible summer." We find our orders and our compass within us. "The more you listen to the voice within you, the better you will hear what is sounding outside," noted Dag Hammarskjold. "I don't know Who — or What — put the question — I don't know when it was put. I don't even remember answering. But at some moment I did answer Yes to Someone — or Something — and from that hour I was certain that existence is meaningful and that, therefore, my life, in self-surrender, had a goal."[1]

I choose to believe that it is God who speaks quietly inside us — that it is he who put the question deep within. And when we answer yes, he reveals the meaning he has chosen for us to enjoy; he unveils the goal that he has been keeping for us all along. I love how Paul puts it in Ephesians 2: "We are God's handiwork, created in Christ Jesus to do good works, which God prepared *in advance* for us to do" (v. 10, italics mine).

In a real football game, you cannot leave halftime and go back to the first half. In life you can. Some do. Others stay in halftime, forever struggling to come up with a new game plan. Still others try to live in the first half but make repeated ventures into the second. They are in a sort of perpetual seismic testing pattern, looking over the ledge but never jumping.

It is time to jump.

In an earlier chapter I advised that you be patient. I hope you don't consider it contradictory to tell you not to be *too* patient. It would be a shame to come this far and then settle back into your first-half game plan. There really is so much more for you to gain by putting one thing in your box and then going for it.

Then why do we hesitate? I have never tried bungee jumping, but I think I know what it must feel like to be perched at the top of a tower and hear the jump master tell me it's time to take the big plunge. In fact, when Mike Kami told me what I had to do after I drew a cross in the box, I knew that the most exhilarating way down would be to jump. Anything else would be climbing back down the ladder to safer, more familiar ground. The jump would be scary, unfamiliar, and, yes, dangerous — but it had the promise of the unforgettable.

I did not want to jump, but I knew that it was time.

My hunch is that you too know it's time, so I will conclude this section with two brief stories — one about a man who knew it was time but decided to climb back down the tower; the other about a man who jumped.

Jim wanted nothing more than to grab the top spot of a major company. He was a real hard-charger who was used to winning, and within a few years he had worked his way up to become the CEO of a large company in Dallas. But the joy was short-lived. Shortly after he reached the top, he was forced to place the company in Chapter 11 bankruptcy. I meet with Jim regularly and, after the company crashed, he began talking about going into teaching or maybe public service. One foot was in halftime, and I could see that he was sincere about making some significant changes in his life. Today, however, he's working harder than ever in an executive job in another large company.

Jim heard the still, small voice say, "It's time," but he didn't listen. He could not bring himself to jump.

Jack was a splendidly successful businessman who had the gift of making more money than he ever could have used up in a lifetime. He loved his work, but as he approached his middle years, he sensed a desire to move from success to significance. His seismic testing and low-cost probes pointed him toward Christian ministry, so he began looking for a way to use his skills and abilities in that area. Over a period of time, he observed that some of his business contacts wanted to serve a higher purpose with their money but just didn't get around to doing it because they didn't have a staff to seek out the opportunities. So Jack began a firm to serve large corporations and wealthy individuals who have the inclination — but not the time — to reinvest their funds in worthy causes. Jack searches for new entrepreneurial ideas and funds them with the excess money generated by his clients. The donors remain anonymous yet get the pleasure of seeing their money at work during their lifetimes.

Jack was at the edge of the bungee-jumping tower, jumped with confidence, and is having the time of his life.

What's stopping you?

PART 3

THE SECOND HALF

If one advances confidently in the direction of his dreams,
and endeavors to live the life which he has imagined,
he will meet with a success unexpected in common hours.
He will pass an invisible boundary; new, universal,
and more liberal laws will begin to establish themselves
around and within him; and he will live with the license
of a higher order of beings.

Henry David Thoreau

CHAPTER 15

Life Mission

What I really lack is to be clear in my mind what I am to do, not what I am to know.... The thing is to understand myself, to see what God really wishes me to do ... to find the idea for which I can live and die.

Søren Kierkegaard

As I approached my middle years, I began to feel that the time was drawing near when I should address concerns and questions that seemed more in the realm of the eternal than the temporal. When I discovered my "one thing," I felt more than ever before in concert with what was intended for my life. I felt that I could, through grace and diligence, live up to the epitaph I had chosen: 100X.

But it is not enough to *feel* like doing something significant. The newly discovered resolve that comes when you place just one thing in the box will fade if you do not apply it to a related goal. Most likely, your first half was filled with good intentions springing from your core beliefs. You wanted to be a better parent, spouse, Christian, and community member; you wanted to leave a positive mark on the world. And you probably lived up to more than a few of these expectations. Yet something was still missing. All of your good intentions somehow could not fulfill that subconscious desire to be more significant than successful.

You had the right instincts but no delivery system.

Lately many businesses and other human organizations have developed mission statements, vision statements, or credos that attempt to explain why their company exists and what it hopes to accomplish. For example:

> MICROSOFT: Your potential. Our passion.
>
> GENERAL ELECTRIC: Imagination at work.
>
> WORLD VISION: Making a better world for children.

When such declarations are well stated, they are usually very simple and easily understood. A mission statement becomes, as a team of consultants once noted in the *Harvard Business Review*, "the magnetic North Pole, the focal point" for that business. Everything the company does points in that direction.

Developing a *personal* mission statement makes a lot of sense, especially for second-halfers. During the first half, you probably either did not have time to develop such a declaration of mission, or the mission statement you adopted really belonged to the company for which you worked. You did not own it, or at least not in the sense that is now possible in the second half.

You will not get very far in your second half without knowing your life mission. Can yours be stated in a sentence or two? A good way to begin formulating one is with some questions (and nakedly honest answers). What is your passion? What have you achieved? What have you done uncommonly well? How are you wired? Where do you belong? What are the "shoulds" that have trailed you during the first half? These and other questions like them will direct you toward the self your heart longs for; they will help you discover the task for which you were especially made.

Stephen R. Covey, author of *The Seven Habits of Highly Effective People*, suggests that in developing a personal mission statement, you should focus on what you wish to be and do, based on the values and principles that undergird all your beliefs and actions. "Whatever is at the center of our life will be the source of our security, guidance, wisdom, and power," writes Covey.[1]

My own mission statement is very short, but yours may be longer. One of the best (and longest) personal mission statements I know of was written by Andrew Carnegie when he was thirty-three years old, about the same age I was when I wrote my six goals for life. Here is what he wrote in his journal as a road map for how he would spend the rest of his days:

> Thirty-three and an income of $50,000 per annum. By this time two years from now I can arrange all my business as to make no effort to increase fortune but spend the surplus each year for benevolent purposes. Settle in Oxford and get a thorough education, making the acquaintance of literary men — this will take three years' active work — pay especial attention to speaking in public. Settle then in London and purchase a controlling interest in some newspaper or live review and give the general management of it attention, taking a part in public matters, especially those connected with education and improvement of the poorer classes. Man must have an idol — the amassing of wealth is one of the worst species of idolatry. No idol more debasing than the worship of money. Whatever I engage in I must push inordinately; therefore I should be careful to choose that life which will be the most elevating in its character. To continue much longer overwhelmed by business cares and with most of my thoughts wholly upon the way to make more money in the shortest time, must degrade me beyond hope of permanent recovery. I will resign business at thirty-five, but during the ensuing two years, I wish to spend the afternoons in securing instruction, and in reading systematically.[2]

Well, it turned out to be three decades — not two years — for

Carnegie's vision of a life of service to come to pass. Even so, in the end his contribution was at least a hundredfold more than his original plan called for. From the time he invested the fruits of his first career in building the steel industry until his death in 1920, Carnegie replanted 90 percent of his fortune.

To show you that not every mission statement must be as long and involved as Carnegie's, I'll share mine. I like to think of myself as a strategic broker — someone who has the skills needed to link problem identifiers with problem solvers. This is how I am wired, and this is what I did with my cable television business, so my life mission necessarily relates to this role. My life mission is: To transform the latent energy in American Christianity into active energy.

This is what I do; it is how I want my life to count. It releases me to be myself — to use gifts that are already there. I do not have to become something that feels uncomfortable or strange. If your own mission statement fits you as well, it will be the right one for you. If it forces you into something that does not fit, it will be someone else's mission.

Closely aligned with your mission statement are your life commitments. One of the consequences of my transition into the second half is that I no longer organize my life in terms of goals. Instead, I now make commitments. These commitments also help me stay focused on my mission, and I share them here not because they are especially profound, but because they might encourage you to develop a list of commitments for your own life mission:

1. The primary loyalty of my life is Jesus Christ. I am committed to fully put into play my gifts in service to him.

2. I am committed to a vital marriage until "death do us part."

3. I have committed the majority of my time and money to

beginning and developing a series of overlapping ventures that release the latent energy in American Christianity.

4. I am committed to be an effective steward of the resources entrusted to my care.

5. I am committed to be a good friend to ten people.

6. I am committed to have a renaissance in the second half of my life.

7. I am committed to practice "altruistic egoism." (Altruistic egoism means gaining personal satisfaction by helping others. It recognizes self-interest as central to my human design, and it counts as greatest gain the goodwill of one's neighbors.)

In addition to the Halftime Assignment on page 191, here is one last tip to help you determine your second-half mission. Peter Drucker suggested that these are the two most important questions in helping you discover the unique role God has prepared beforehand for you to walk in. The questions are:

What have you achieved? (competence)

What do you care deeply about? (passion)

The goal is to find something that fits within the boundaries of these two questions — something you're good at and that really excites you. You may be good at working with people yet care passionately about solitude. If you sell out to the first, the other will work against you. But if you look deeply enough inside of you and are honest about *combining* your competence with your passion, you will find the mission that is best suited to you.

In addition to the Halftime Assignment on page 191, an excellent resource to help you discover your life mission is the book *What Color Is Your Parachute?* by Dick Bolles. An ordained Episcopal priest, Bolles began his journey with *Parachute* when he was let go by his church in San Francisco, probably the best thing that could have happened to him, though it must not have seemed so at the time. Over the years since the book was first released, Bolles has updated and revised it, and the current edition includes a section called "How to Find Your Mission in Life."[3]

Today, tomorrow, certainly by the end of next week, set aside some time to spend with a pencil and a sheet of paper — maybe several sheets. Make lists: things to do in your second half, things you are committed to, slogans and creeds that reflect the true you, statements that combine what you believe with what you want to do with the rest of your life.

After you have made your lists, pray. Read what you have written. Reflect. Listen. Share what you have written with your spouse and with a small group of friends. Then put the paper away in a drawer. Pray some more. Listen a lot. Think about what you love to do most, and let these thoughts roll gently through your soul like lazy waves on the ocean. This is the stuff that you never took the time to do in the first half — enjoy it!

In a week or so, get out a clean sheet of paper. Write these words at the top: "My Life Mission."

I think you know what to do next.

CHAPTER 16

Regaining Control

Unless a person takes charge of them,
both work and free time are likely to be disappointing.
Mihály Csíkszentmihályi

A friend of mine who had been president of a large publishing company once sought out a world-renowned Zen master. After unloading the tremendous business of his life onto the master without provoking much response, he decided to be quiet for a moment. The Zen master began to pour tea into a beautiful oriental teacup until it overflowed the cup and spread across the grass mat toward my friend. Bewildered, my friend asked the Zen master what he was doing. The Zen master replied: "Your life is like a teacup, flowing over. There's no room for anything new. You need to pour out, not take more in."

There are two kinds of capital that each of us has to spend. *Economic capital* is the money and time for leisure that you earn by working. For the most part, it is spent on living requirements and luxuries. *Social capital* is the time, money, and knowledge you have available to reinvest or spend in the community that nurtures you.

While most people think of spending money in "the pursuit of happiness," the concept of social capital basically says that the Lord has issued to each of us a portion of time, talent, and treasure to be invested in pursuing instead the first and greatest commandment, "Love the Lord your God with all your heart and with all your soul and with all your mind," and the second greatest commandment, "Love your neighbor as yourself" (Matthew 22:37, 39).

The payoff for investment of social capital is blessedness. This shouldn't be surprising. After all, perhaps the truest and most practical of Jesus' teachings is that "it is more blessed to give than to receive" (Acts 20:35). What a difference it might have made had Thomas Jefferson reworded the Declaration of Independence to read "life, liberty, and the pursuit of *blessedness*"!

One major objective of an effective halftime and second half is to create capacity. Referring back to the story at the beginning of this chapter, my cup too was running over. I needed to create capacity by recapturing the majority of my time and by converting a good portion of my net worth into liquid funds to be invested for social purposes. I needed to transform my economic capital into social capital.

If you have followed the mutual funds market, you are probably familiar with the name Peter Lynch. Peter was a terrific example of someone who transformed economic capital into social capital. As portfolio manager for Fidelity Investments' Magellan Fund, he took the fund from twenty million to fourteen *billion* dollars in his thirteen-year tenure at its helm. He had it all. Great job. Great family. Great satisfaction from working with charities. Yet at age forty-six, he decided to put boundaries on the time he was willing to spend at his job so that he could assume greater control over his life.

Lynch had come to the realization that eventually overtakes all of us: *I can't keep living like this.* It's not that what he was doing was so bad. In fact, it was all very good. But, as he explained, "For me it was like hot-fudge sundaes: How much can you handle without getting a stomachache?" His new schedule allowed him to leave home after his kids left for school. He works four days a week (two for Fidelity and two for charity), and Mondays he allocates entirely to his wife.

You don't have to be the CEO of a major investment company to be able to change the way you work. The wireless, virtual text-message, voicemail, and email environment we live in now means we are no longer chained to a physical office. We can talk to anyone from anyplace, night or day. Now more than ever it is more possible to negotiate a work schedule that allows you to be home when your kids need you the most.

Most first-halfers become victims of centrifugal force. Around the perimeter of their lives are vital points that demand attention: family, work, community involvement (service clubs, local school, etc.), church, professional development, leisure activities, and avocations. They begin with every good intention of tending to each, but to do that, they have to shift into a higher gear. Before long they are spinning rapidly around the perimeter, the resulting force driving them farther and farther from the center, the core of who they are. At that point, all control has been lost.

The second half is about regaining control of your life — about calling your own shots. Do you think it was easy for Peter Lynch to tell his colleagues at Fidelity Investments that he was no longer going to manage their most profitable and visible fund? He was able to do it because he knew that being unable to control his work life would sooner or later result in a major loss in the other important areas of his life.

Getting back to the center requires us to downshift, to slow down. And once we return to the core — once we know who we are and what's in the box — we can accept the fact that some of the things on the perimeter will not receive as much attention as they once did. Some things will be more important than others; some may need to be ignored altogether. But regardless of what stays and what gets tossed aside, the point is that we no longer let someone else decide that for us. We create capacity for the things that matter.

If this sounds radical or out of step with the way things generally work, it is because baby boomers are the first generation to enjoy the luxury of choosing what they do with their second half, changing the playing field for subsequent generations. Your parents were probably very much like my father-in-law, who worked as a senior executive with an international oil supply company until he retired. It was important for him to stay the course in order to get the medical, dental, and postretirement benefits that come with long service to a large, hierarchical company. As well, most people in our parents' generation had what author Charles Handy calls "employment work": full-time salary jobs with attractive benefits packages in good-sized companies.

That's not the way it's going to be in the future. Every day newspapers report how big companies are laying off more and more people — both blue- and white-collar workers. "Downsizing," "rightsizing," and "reengineering" are the current buzzwords of the corporate environment. The upside of this is that many of those who were let go are now working as independent contractors, working on a contract basis with their former employer as well as with other companies. In fact, you may be one of those independent contractors, which will give you much more flexibility in your second half. Most job growth today is in firms that have fewer than one hundred employees — a great part of the growth in firms with fewer than twenty employees! Peter Drucker believed that one of the major reasons for the growth of these smaller firms is that leaders could become their own bosses and call more of their own shots.

In his book *The Age of Unreason*, Charles Handy asserts that in the future people will spend only about half of their working hours in employment organizations, with the remaining half spent in what he calls "portfolio work" — part-time work, consulting work, and temporary work for a variety of employers.[1] My cable television company, for example, built 4,500 miles of cable television in about two years, using almost entirely small-firm subcontractors to obtain the franchises, map the systems, construct the cable, market the subscribers, and get the systems installed.

All of these trends make it increasingly possible for anyone to make the changes that are necessary to have a significant second half. People will be freer to choose what they do than ever before, allowing them to discard the work-related activities that force them to run at full speed all the time.

Still, having a fruitful second half is more than just slowing down or being able to control your calendar. It has to do with a mind-set, an inner compass that is fixed on those things that define the true self. Psychologist Mihály Csíkszentmihályi spent twenty-five years trying to figure out what makes people happy. He discovered that happiness is not something that just happens. Neither does it have much to do with money, power, or material possessions, as evidenced by the fact that happiness can be found among both rich and poor, powerful and weak. Says Csíkszent-mihályi, "People who control inner experience will be able to determine the quality of their lives, which is as close as any of us can come to being happy."[2]

I do not know if Mr. Csíkszentmihályi is a Christian or not, but there is much in the Christian faith that supports his discovery. Our Lord taught us to be like children (carefree), not to worry so much (not be controlled by needs and possessions), and to avoid being controlled by many masters. And in Paul's letter to the church in Rome, the apostle explains the importance of controlling the inner being in order to have a fulfilling life: "Those who live according to the sinful nature have their minds set on what that nature desires; but those who live in accordance with the Spirit have their minds set on what the Spirit desires.

The mind controlled by the sinful nature is death, but the mind controlled by the Spirit is life and peace" (Romans 8:5–6).

The irony here is that the church has become one of those masters under which many first-halfers feel hopelessly indentured. The joy that ought to come from serving others in Christ's name is missing because so much of what we do for the church is done out of a spirit of obligation and involves doing work that is far removed from our core competencies. And that is because, as first-halfers, we have not yet discovered who we are, what we really enjoy doing, and how even the most undesirable task can be a freeing, exhilarating experience if it arises out of our core being. For most people, church work is not like a hot-fudge sundae but is like the broccoli and spinach your mother made you eat as a child.

Once you have discovered your life's mission, you are in a much better position to regain control over well-intentioned ministry efforts. Instead of dragging your feet to yet another "witnessing weekend," for example, you could decide to allow the light of your faith to shine through naturally on the golf course, at the gym, or having lunch with friends from work. This way you have regained control in a way that brings together your desire to serve God, your love for a card game, and your need to enjoy a night out with like-minded individuals.

It is encouraging to see how some churches are becoming better at matching passion with talent. Robert Bellah, coauthor of the bestselling *Habits of the Heart*, calls this a function of "mediating institutions."[3] Hundreds of churches are adding "volunteer resources directors" or "linking teams" to help people discover how to apply their best selves to invigorating ministry through the church. For example, Mariners Church in Orange County, California, consistently places more than five thousand members in useful volunteer work in surrounding communities. Willow Creek Community Church in the Chicago suburbs has developed a program called Network (now published and used by many churches nationwide) to help people discern their individual design and to help place them in appropriate volunteer work. Saddleback Valley Community Church in Mission Viejo, California, helps people find their S.H.A.P.E.:

> **S**piritual gifts
> **H**eart, passions
> **A**bilities
> **P**ersonality
> **E**xperience, "know-how"

If Christian second-halfers are to make any progress in seeing their life missions become reality, more and more churches will have to adopt this approach to getting people involved. My own ministry, Leadership Network, developed the Leadership Training Network, a program that sponsored five-day training institutes for volunteer resource directors in churches. We eventually passed that on to Sue Mallory, who developed the program, and it is now part of the Church Volunteer Association (*www.Church-VolunteerCentral.com*), the largest association of volunteer leadership, with nearly ten thousand participating churches.

Practical Matters

It is one thing to talk about regaining control yet quite another to really do it. Old habits, even tempered with a brand-new outlook on life, die hard. Here are some things I have done to regain control over my own destiny:

Delegate — at work, play, and home. You cannot do everything and shouldn't try. This becomes especially important for those whose second half involves keeping their present job but doing it at "half speed." Work smarter, not harder.

Do what you do best; drop the rest. I tend to be a visionary, so

I'm less motivated to do hands-on implementation, though I can and have done it. Not anymore. Go with your strengths.

Know when to say no. The more successful you are, the more you will be asked to help others. Don't let others talk you into doing something you don't want to do or don't have time to do; it will become a chore. You want to pursue your mission, not someone else's.

Set limits. If you currently keep an average of four appointments a day, cut back to two or three. If you normally stay an hour after work, go home on time. If you take twelve business trips a year, cut back to six or eight. Reallocate time to your mission, to your core issues.

Protect your personal time by putting it on your calendar. I like Ken Blanchard's advice to start your day slow. It is much easier to maintain control over your life if you have a regular quiet time. This time should be more than devotions, though it ought to include prayer and Bible reading. Leave time for absolute silence, for deliberately looking at your life to see that it is in balance. This is probably the most vital activity for me in terms of staying in control.

Work with people you like. One of my friends, Karol Emmerich, who quit several years ago as treasurer of Dayton-Hudson, says, "I want to find all the people I like being with and find some beneficial work we can do together. In my second half, I want to work with people who add energy to life, not with those who take energy away."

Set timetables. Your mission is important and therefore deserving of your attention and care. If you do not put your second-half dreams on a timetable, they will quickly become unfulfilled wishes.

Downsize. When Thoreau moved into a cabin on Walden Pond, he lightened up on the nonessentials in his life. Think about all the time and energy that are drained by owning a boat, a cottage, a second or third car, or a country club membership. None of these things are bad by themselves and are, in fact, designed to provide some fun in your life, but they can very easily become master controllers. Most people I know who own a boat feel they have to use it to make it a worthwhile investment. I also know people who do not particularly enjoy spending four hours on a golf course but do it because they belong to a club. If these kinds of things stand between you and regaining control of your life, get rid of them.

Play around a little. Not in the sense that would get you in trouble, but as a way to keep a handle on who's in charge. There is something about skipping out of work to catch a baseball game in the middle of the week or taking your spouse to a movie instead of attending a church committee meeting that reminds you who is calling the shots. Play ought to be a big second-half activity, not so much in terms of time spent, but in importance.

Take the phone off the hook. Not literally (at least not all the time), but learn how to hide gracefully. I don't always like talking to voicemail when I call someone, but I wouldn't live without voicemail myself. It lets *me* control who I talk to and when. Cell phones are great because you can call someone when you need to then shut off the phone and ride in wondrous silence. Unless you're a brain surgeon on twenty-four-hour call, I don't think it's necessary to let people know where you are all the time.

I have also learned, from the wonderful coaching of Peter Drucker, three cardinal principles that guide our work at Leadership Network and help me keep control over my life:

Build on the islands of health and strength. This is very counterintuitive for philanthropy, which tends to seek to help the helpless. Building on health and strength, however, is a better idea in that it builds independence rather than dependence.

Work only with those who are receptive to what you are trying to do. You have only a limited amount of time. Trying to convince people to do what they really don't want to do uses four times the amount of energy required to help others conceive or implement their own ideas.

Work only on things that will make a great deal of difference if you succeed. This is a mission, not a hobby. Why invest all your time and energy in something that will only bring incremental change. Aim high!

Desire alone will not allow you to do something new in your second half; you must create the capacity to do it. If you are being controlled by too many time- and energy-consuming activities, you will continue to be frustrated by unfulfilled dreams and desires. Realize, too, that you are in unfamiliar territory, and it may take some practice before you feel comfortable. Eventually, however, you will find a way to regain control of your own life.

CHAPTER 17

Healthy Individualism

Let's just go ahead and be what we were made to be,
without enviously or pridefully comparing ourselves with each other,
or trying to be something we aren't.
Romans 12:3 MSG

I know many people who believe — honestly believe — that giving your life over to Christ and to the church is antithetical to the ideals and character of individualism. They look upon Christians and churchgoers as conformists, and probably mindless ones to boot. In fact, you may have become a little uncomfortable in the previous chapter when I urged you to take control of your life, to become your own master, because as a Christian you have been taught that submission to Christ means "dying to self."

This is a heresy, and a dangerous one at that. In Christ's church, individualism is amplified, encouraged, supported, and complemented. We each are grafted to a body that needs our strengths and compensates for our weaknesses by matching them with the gifts of other members of the body. The image of a weak, wimpy follower is not supported in Scripture. Paul urges Timothy to "be strong." He counsels him to "fan into flame the gift of God, which is in you.... For the Spirit God gave us does not make us timid, but gives us power, love and self-discipline" (2 Timothy 1:6–7). The images Paul sets before Timothy are those of a soldier enduring hardship, an athlete in training, and a hard-laboring farmer — all brawny, manly individuals.

Those who frown on individualism are telling only half the gospel story. The well-intentioned (and biblically correct) doctrine of depravity is not the whole story. Without God we are, indeed, in need of "amazing grace," but once we are transformed by his grace, we become new, beautiful, and valuable creatures capable of self-love as well as self-control.

I think the reason why so many Christians have accepted the conformist label is that we see so much *unhealthy* individualism in society, especially in the pathological individualism of the baby boomers, but also in the dipped-in-irony self-centeredness of today's postmodern generation. This type of individualism (which is not limited to a particular generation, by the way) leads to selfish isolation, alienation, greed, callousness, and guilt. When Jesus talks about dying to self, I believe he is talking about dying to this "me first" pathological self-worship, not the uniquely created self that he has given us.

The Small Self and the Large Self

Much of our first-half misery can be traced back to a preoccupation with self. In the second half, you break free from yourself. While the first-half self is small, the second-half self is large. The first-half self winds inward, wrapping tighter and tighter around itself. The second-half self winds outward, unraveling itself from the paralysis of a tightly wound spring.

The small self contains only you. It is basically alienated, alone, and pathologically individualistic. The larger self is whole because it is bonded with something transcendent. Self-transcendence has legs; it goes the distance and completes the race.

The Bible relates many instances of the small self. One such example is the parable of the rich fool. Here is a man who had

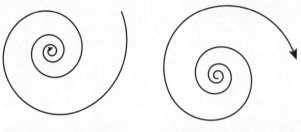

FIRST-HALF SELF   SECOND-HALF SELF

achieved great success, so much that he had to build bigger barns to contain all his treasures. (I see him as a real first-half go-getter, with a house in a pricey subdivision that's too small to hold all his toys.) Yet Jesus called him a fool, saying, "This very night your life will be demanded from you. Then who will get what you have prepared for yourself?" Then Jesus added, "This is how it will be with those who store up things for themselves but are not rich toward God" (Luke 12:20–21). The rich fool is small and miserly. He is trapped within the little self.

But the Bible is also filled with images of the larger self: the man who knows himself and his mission so well that he will lay down his life for his brother. Think about the Samaritan, whose large self overcame the stigma of doing something out of the ordinary. Or how about John the Baptist, who, very much a man who did things his own way, paid the ultimate price for following a cause? And remember the widow who gave out of her poverty, gave everything because she knew who she was and what was in the box?

You too can be a great example if you can make the distinction between your small self and your large self. Sacrificing your immediate self, the small self, for a larger gain is what Jesus meant when he talked about the cost of following him — giving up your tightly wound selfishness to gain something bigger, better. People are at their largest, their noblest and most virtuous, when they are given over to a cause, something larger than themselves.

Individual Teammates

Each of us is designed by our Creator to be incomplete. As we grow up, we grow from a state of dependence as small children to one of independence as adolescents and adults. Independence feels great, but it is not the final stage. Beyond independence, we have yet to reach the stage of interdependence — the stage where we understand and accept that we cannot accomplish anything significant on our own.

The apostle Paul expresses this best in his letter to the Corinthian church, in which he uses the analogy of the body:

> Just as a body, though one, has many parts, but all its many parts form one body, so it is with Christ.... Now if the foot should say, "Because I am not a hand, I do not belong to the body," it would not for that reason cease to be part of the body. And if the ear should say, "Because I am not an eye, I do not belong to the body," it would not for that reason cease to be part of the body. If the whole body were an eye, where would the sense of hearing be? If the whole body were an ear, where would the sense of smell be? But in fact God has placed the parts in the body, every one of them, just as he wants them to be. If they were all one part, where would the body be? As it is, there are many parts, but one body. The eye cannot say to the hand, "I don't need you!" (1 Corinthians 12:12, 15–21)

I cannot recall a single thing worth doing that I've accomplished by myself. The individualism in the Bible is the individualism of an eye or a foot — a part that functions as part of a larger, harmonious whole. The individualism so rampant in our culture is a first-half individualism that borders on selfishness; its focus is almost always personal gain. Second-half individualism always finds its strength in concert with others of like-minded vision. I learned long ago to build on my own strength and natural giftedness and to depend on others with complementary strengths to make the work I'm doing complete.

The Selfishness of Altruism

Several years ago I had the distinct privilege of hearing a remarkable man who was at that time the world's leading expert on stress. Hans Selye was a microbiologist from Canada who coined a phrase that sounded almost contradictory: altruistic egoism. As Selye explained it, and as I learned more about it from his landmark book *The Stress of Life*, altruistic egoism is nothing more than the biblical truth that helping others helps *you*.[1] Selye had learned that those who earn the goodwill of their neighbors are dramatically better off psychologically and physiologically than those who are looked upon as selfish and greedy.

Selye wrote that the best way to earn the goodwill of your neighbor is to ask either explicitly or implicitly, "What can I do to be useful to you?" And then, if possible, to do it. I can't explain it, but this works for me. And in all the times I have asked this question, I cannot recall a single occasion when someone took advantage of me. Instead, people are stunned by the rarity and vulnerability of the question. And most of the time, I really can do something that is useful, and often it does not require money or very much time.

Fred Smith Sr., a long-time Christian leader and author, told me years ago that being a Christian has to do with learning to do by reflex action that which you first learn to do by duty and discipline. Asking, "Is there anything I can do to be useful to you?" and then doing it is something I learned first by duty. Then, after much practice, it became a reflex action.

For example, I was once in a small group with Jerry Mays, a contractor who was an all-pro linebacker for the Kansas City Chiefs years ago. Jerry was a "gentle giant" who gradually wasted away from cancer with incredible courage and dignity right before our eyes. At one point, I sent Jerry a small lamb and cross sculpture I owned that is a replica of a piece in the Vatican collection. In turn, he sent me one of the most touching and encouraging letters I've ever received, saying that he observed Christlikeness in my behavior. He promised to look my son, Ross, up when he got to heaven. Obviously, the sculpture brought some joy into Jerry's life, but it is impossible to describe the inner joy I experienced in reading his letter to me. It *is* more blessed to give than to receive!

This fleshed-out "neighbor love" offers practical, tangible benefits as well. Consider this report that first appeared in the Roman Catholic magazine *Liguorian*:

> Medical researchers are now finding scientific proof for what Jesus taught so long ago, that giving of self to others is actually a form of receiving (Acts 20:35). This seeming contradiction finds meaning only when seen through the eyes of Christ. Not only are scientists proving this paradox to be true, they further assert that helping others is good for your health.... A study done at the University of Michigan revealed that persons who regularly volunteer their time heighten their overall zest for living and increase their life expectancy. Studies on the aging process have reached a similar conclusion.... Stress researchers from the University of Illinois found that persons who feel connected with other people are more calm, less tense.... Giving can be disguised in many forms, from understanding to empathy, from compassion to acts of service. Whatever it takes, the core is still the same — giving of ourselves is offering love, and love remains the only gift that multiplies when you give it away.

I have read that sometimes people suffering from emotional illness are given a "prescription" to do acts of service or kindness for others because it helps them rise above their own problems.

I know this is true because, in the weeks after Ross was lost, I found that the only thing that would bring me "temporary symptomatic relief" (like the promise on the backs of aspirin boxes) was to become mentally engaged in helping someone else. Going out of my way to help someone made me feel better. That is why it is so important to have a cause, a mission, in your second half: not only is it a decoy for your emotional system in order to keep you busy; it is also the key that unlocks the door to your larger self.

I am convinced that part of the secret to a better second half is a proper understanding of self-love. Success in the first half is lonely because it is directed inward. It gains significance in the second half from the "pouring out" of ourselves, our gifts, our talents, our resources. As you begin to hit your stride in the second half, pay attention to yourself.

Here are some "road signs" to alert you to your own sense of individualism:

Healthy individualism	Unhealthy individualism
Part of a team	Arrogant and alone
With God (rich toward God)	Without God
Working from your strengths	Functioning in your weakness
Able to confess	Stuck with shame and guilt
Self-realization and community	More success = more isolation = less community

CHAPTER 18

Lifelong Learning

With all thy getting, get understanding.
**An adaptation of Proverbs 4:7 as quoted every month
for years in the back of *Forbes* magazine**

I only really became a student after I finished school. I suspect that is true for most of us. When we were in high school and college, we were not students, but clients. Education was a means to an end; it provided a union card to allow us to work in the closed shop of productive life. Public service announcements urge kids to stay in school so that they can get into college or get good jobs. I do not recall hearing announcements that told me to stay in school so that I could learn the meaning of life or gain an appreciation for the depth of insight in classical literature.

I am not being critical of our educational system. It is geared for the first half. We demand that it teach us how to work, how to have careers, and how to be successful. For the most part, it delivers; it equips us to be productive. We do not ask much more of education until we get to halftime, the point at which we finally begin to understand that life becomes richer when we are students and narrows when we stop learning.

A friend of mine told me about a man he met on a plane who had been in college for fourteen years. He was not a "terminal student," seeking a number of degrees, nor was he in an extended training program related to his career. This man was a mechanic who was being sent by his company to a job at another factory and had been a mechanic since he graduated from high school. For several years he welded steel boxes of various sizes together, taking pride in his work. Then he saw an advertisement in the newspaper for a local community college that listed its course offerings, which would be starting in a few weeks. He signed up for a biology class because he liked the outdoors, and he got hooked. He now speaks two languages besides English and has the equivalent of a B.A. in English. He has also taken classes in physics, music, religion, and history. And he still welds boxes together.

It would be easy to dismiss this guy as someone who is indulging himself in some nonutilitarian luxury, but something about him appeals to me. Why should all learning have a utilitarian purpose? Why not learn a new language just because you would like to speak and read German or French, not because it is a requirement for a degree or because you need to do business in Germany? This man had discovered the joy of learning, something that he did not discover until after high school. His is a second-half approach to the glorious world of knowledge.

Why Learning Is Important in the Second Half

There are some obvious reasons why it is important to continue learning in the second half. If learning prepares you to deal positively and productively with change, then it is more important now than ever before. In my brief lifetime, for example, I have seen the treatment of minority groups go from "back of the bus" segregationist policies to the mandated quotas of multiculturalism. One does not adjust to that without learning.

I have had seven jobs in my professional career, and in my current role as a strategic broker, the playing field is constantly shifting. I cannot fulfill my mission unless I am engaged in a fairly systematic, or at least consistent, pattern of learning.

Another reason to learn in the second half is to "unlearn" the doctrine of specialization. Most first-halfers are trained in the language and operations of their particular field. Accountants stay current on tax laws but know little about management theory; a neurosurgeon may have progressed from scalpel to laser to nuclear probes but would be hard-pressed to treat a gunshot wound. Second-half missions tend to be more holistic and demand a more widely rounded practitioner.

There is also the very practical issue of staying sharp. Senility (not to be confused with Alzheimer's disease) is, I am told, no longer felt to be an inevitable condition of aging. Most gerontologists subscribe to the "use it or lose it" theory when it comes to mental alertness. I have seen too many men and women let their minds grow fallow as they approach their sixties. I do not want it to happen to me, and it does not have to happen to you. Working with Peter Drucker through his mideighties and with the delightfully youthful Frances Hesselbein during the early years of the Peter Drucker Foundation for Nonprofit Management has shown me what a vital, energetic, and productive season the years after "retirement age" can be.

But perhaps the most compelling reason for nurturing an active mind comes from my admittedly nontechnical interpretation of the New Testament account of Jesus casting out a demon in Luke 11:24–26. Jesus said that when an evil spirit returns to an individual and "finds the house swept clean," it enters that house with even more evil spirits because there is so much room to fill.

I think the key theme here is emptiness, and I don't think it is too much of a stretch to suggest that if we let our minds become empty, they can be filled with much that detracts us from the mission of our second half. One way or another, our minds will indeed be filled with something. I shudder to think what kind of person I would be today if I had given myself a steady diet of talk shows, soap operas, tabloid journalism, and the like. For this reason alone, we ought to be diligent in learning good and wholesome things to protect our minds from the debasing things that are so easily absorbed. This is also why I consider studying the Bible to be a valid form of lifelong learning. If "garbage in, garbage out" is true, then the reverse must be true also.

What to Learn in the Second Half

It is impossible to design a curriculum for everyone's second half, but I generally apply this rule: You only really learn what you need and are willing to act on; the rest is amusement and passing the time away. In other words, you learn best when the subjects you are studying in some way apply to what is important to you and your second-half mission.

This rule suggests that the welder I referred to earlier was merely amusing himself, though I have no way of knowing just how he used his knowledge. There is nothing inherently wrong with that — the pure joy of learning could be, for some people, an end in itself. With all the inane things people do to enjoy themselves, signing up for a Spanish class looks pretty good. But if you are learning with no particular goal in mind — whether stated or loosely understood — you will eventually come to view learning as a pastime. I recommend focusing on those things that will help you accomplish your mission but keeping a creative and liberal view of just what that could include.

For example, I study art. I allow myself to purchase inexpensive art books so that I can cut out a reproduction of an important painting and push-pin it up on a cork board in my closet, where I will see it each morning and evening while I dress. I visit museums and galleries whenever I have the chance, and I have a modest collection of art in my home. I would be hard-pressed to make a direct connection between my study of art and my work as a Christian philanthropist, other than to show that I believe in the power of art to inspire. A Japanese scholar of several centuries ago said, "Great art captures the spirit of a thing." When I look at a painting, I am moved by the beauty or power or emotion of the piece; I learn something about myself and the world — about the human condition. For me that's enough "permission" to include art in my goal of lifelong learning.

Because so much of what I do revolves around human organizations, I also take advantage of seminars, workshops, conferences, and study programs in the areas of business, management, leadership, and related subjects. Likewise, your second-half learning program should include formal and informal learning in areas that represent the "hands on" aspect of your life mission. If you are an attorney and have decided to cut back on work for your firm so that you can provide some pro bono legal counsel to urban ministries, it would make sense to stay current in nonprofit legal issues. Or let's say you are a public school teacher who has taken advantage of early retirement incentives being offered in many districts, and you feel called to set up a study skills center through your local church. Since you will probably need to recruit volunteers to help staff the center, it might be worthwhile to interview an official from your local United Way or other charitable organization to learn the dynamics of volunteerism.

The mistake most people make when they move into the second half is to rely on good intentions. If, at some point, you become discouraged by lack of progress in your life mission, it is possible that you simply may not have gained the knowledge and information necessary to support your dream.

How to Learn in the Second Half

In many ways, everything you do in the second half is a form of learning. That is because learning is really just adopting an attitude of discovery. Expect to learn from everything you approach and don't get too hung up on trying to formalize your study. To show you just how diverse the delivery systems are, I list here those that have been helpful to me and others:

Formal classroom. Our example of the welder would not be a bad one to emulate. I have, from time to time, enrolled in classes to study something that was either interesting or would help me in my mission. There is a definite benefit to the discipline of a systematic program of study, and the nice thing about going to school when you're in your forties is that the pressure to compete is gone. You already have a job, so instead of pressing to get a grade, you do your best to learn something. In most cases, you will end up with one of the higher grades anyway (or if you want, you can audit the course and not worry about grades).

Listening and asking. This is probably my most consistent way of learning things. I just ask. Or sometimes I don't have to ask; I just listen to those around me. If you're a business traveler, you already know how much you can learn (and how easy it is to network) on planes.

Alternative and international media. All media has a spin on it. If your only source of news is the conventional media (network television, daily newspapers, and news magazines), you'll get a slanted picture — not necessarily a false one, but a slanted one. Supplement your standard fare with specialized magazines, cable and satellite television, and the myriad of viewpoints and resources found by surfing the Web. Listen to National Public Radio and read magazines like *The New Republic*, *New Perspectives Quarterly*, *American Demographics*, *Utne Reader*, *The Atlantic*, *The Wilson Quarterly*, *Wired*, and others. The *Wall Street Journal* and *Forbes* are more than business publications. You may not agree with all of them, but isn't that part of learning?

Books. Read voraciously and widely, fiction as well as nonfiction. Read Christian and secular books. Form a book study group to gain other perspectives on the book you're reading.

Every fall and spring, I participate in a course in the classics with a group of fellow lifelong learners.

Audio books and e-books. This is probably a holdover from my first-half days, but I "read" a lot of books while dressing, driving, and exercising, and as electronic reading devices become more user-friendly, downloading e-books makes a lot of sense. The Teaching Company has collected top college lecturers in its Superstar Teachers Series. Most publishing companies offer audio versions of their books, and the audio section of bookstores, both brick and mortar and online, is growing.

Conferences. Well-run conferences can be better than a semester class at a university. Pick up CDs or MP3s from the sessions you can't attend. Keep the notes and handouts for reference.

Interview people. I am amazed at how easy it is to approach someone and ask for an interview. Once they know you're not a reporter, most people are happy to give you a few minutes. Just make sure you're prepared, and don't overextend your allotted time. They say you are only two phone calls away from anyone on earth. It's true.

Travel. One of the greatest forms of education is travel. Linda and I now make it a practice to travel to and do in-depth study into a different region of the world at least once a year. A new trend among second-halfers is "vacation with a purpose." A trip can combine geography, religion, politics, anthropology, art, and music in one comfortable package.

Television. You would expect this from a guy who worked in television, but I honestly believe that TV can be a great vehicle for learning. The average television viewer now has access to over two hundred channels, 24/7. With a DVR that captures and stores one hundred hours of programming, I find that aside from news and sports, I seldom watch anything live anymore. I watch what I want when I want.

Team learning. Bestselling author and MIT professor Peter

Senge says, "Teams, not individuals, are the fundamental learning unit in modern organizations."[1] God seems to have built a governor against arrogance into the design of human beings. We are as interdependent in learning as we are in other areas. After I have thought about some problem by myself for a while, I always find it necessary to enter a give-and-take dialogue with others. It's a way to find the other pieces of the whole puzzle.

The Internet. The Internet can be a tremendous source for learning, and if you are Internet savvy, you can benefit from the information that is literally at your fingertips. One word of caution: whenever so much information is available in one easy-to-access source, issues of reliability and trust come into play. In other words, just because something is on the Internet doesn't mean it's true.

One of the great tragedies of civilization is the transformation that takes place in a child's attitude toward learning. At some point in the schooling process, he or she passes from childlike eagerness toward learning to a passive resistance toward gaining knowledge. Perhaps it is inevitable. What I am proposing, however, is that a person really can reclaim an excitement for learning. Second-half excitement for learning shows that you are unashamed to admit you don't know everything and that you want to learn more. It's acknowledging that "professional" is more of a title or label than a measure of knowledge. In your second half, be willing to become an amateur in a field you haven't mastered.

CHAPTER 19

Respect for Externals

All results are on the outside.
The inside is only cost and effort.
Peter Drucker

Second-half people are a lot like bassoonists.

Think about it. A bassoonist is not very effective outside the context of an orchestra. Trumpeters, violinists, and pianists can all go solo; the bassoonist, for the most part, cannot. And the few bassoon solos that have been written were meant to be performed with an orchestra or ensemble.

Bassoonists who do not accept this reality would be frustrated to the point of either quitting or trying to generate some public interest in a solo bassoon performance. Fortunately, bassoonists have generally accepted their lot in life and have provided listeners with countless hours of wonderful music complemented by their distinctive bass tones.

This analogy illustrates two important facts about second-halfers. First, we are secure enough to be team players. And second, we recognize the need to respect externals — to be at peace with those things that we cannot change and that will be with us forever.

My cable television executive team spent about 25 percent of its review time each month looking at external conditions: regulatory changes, changes in customer responses to some-

one else's offers, changes in culture, new technologies, and demographic changes. They didn't waste their time figuring out
ways to change those external conditions, because they knew
they couldn't. External conditions may become opportunities or
threats to your organization, but one thing is certain: they will
always be with you.

That is not something we learn in our first-half climb. Wind-
mills are for tilting, and tilt we must. Often, the first-half approach to externals is either relentless attack or denial. But there
is a fine line between ambition and stubbornness. One of the
things that put you in halftime was the realization that you
weren't making any headway by constantly butting heads with
external conditions over which you had no control.

In the second half, you learn not just to accept the external
conditions but to respect them, for it is through respect that you
begin to creatively find ways to turn those externals into opportunities. The best example of this is Microsoft, the software
maker. Not so many years ago, everyone wanted to stake a claim
on the computer mother lode, so companies sprang up overnight
and began making computers. And a lot of them made big money.
Bill Gates surveyed the scene and saw IBM rising like a huge
skyscraper. He knew they would always be the biggest player;
that was an external condition he accepted and respected. So instead of aiming his little spear at this huge windmill, he headed
off in another direction; and the rest, as they say, is history. Who
would have thought that a company worth about one-tenth the
value of IBM would one day surpass its value? And what might
have happened if Bill Gates had decided to try to build hardware
to compete with IBM?

Sometimes the externals are so close they almost devour you.
It almost happened to me. I became involved in a venture that
took me out of my league, out of my comfort zone. My partner knew that we had to do something to compete with cable

and began pressuring me to run some soft porn — actually, it was more hard than soft. I was under a lot of stress because, of course, I did not want to have anything to do with pornography. I was also dealing with the added pressure of running a business that was in danger of failing. You see, the porn might have added new viewers and given us needed revenue, but I refused to allow it. And it was a decision that kept the financial thumbscrews cranked down pretty hard.

I remember trying to teach a Sunday school class in the midst of all this. The lesson was from 1 Corinthians 13, and believe me, I was not feeling like anything that was described in that well-known chapter on love. It must have shown, because afterward a guy in the class came up to me and said, "You know, the last time I felt the way you just described, I was a fighter pilot in Korea. Have you ever considered that maybe it isn't work that's getting to you, but the work you're doing?"

He was 100 percent correct. What I needed to do was accept the external reality: I did not belong in that business. I could stay in and fight to my dying day, but some things would never change. So I got out on February 12, 1982, the date that marks the beginning of my second half. It was my big plunge, and I know it was the right thing to do.

The Role of Authority

There is no such thing as a life without authority. You can choose the game, but you can't choose the rules.

If you're going to play tennis, you have to serve behind the line and keep the ball within the sidelines. If your sport is basketball, you must dribble the ball up the court instead of running with it. Simply put, when you choose the game, you inherit its rules. And whether you like it or not, the rules govern your behavior. Follow the rules and your chances of winning are greater.

Break the rules enough times and you won't even get a chance to finish the game.

It must have been a first-halfer who said, "Rules were made to be broken." On the way up the ladder, there is always the temptation to skip a step, to take a shortcut. And there is something about submitting to authority that seems wimpy to many in the first half. The reason auto insurance rates are higher for young people is because it has been proven that they tend not to respect the authority of traffic laws. They speed more, take more chances, and tend to fool themselves into thinking they are immune to authority. First-halfers operate in much the same manner. Although outright rebellion is rare, many first-halfers take the "don't touch the stove" warning as an invitation to push authority's limits.

The problem for the first-halfer is this: you need that job to survive. You may not like it, you may not respect your boss, you may not have agreed with the way the company does things — but you can't just up and leave. At least not very easily. Who'll pay the rent and buy the groceries? You are forced, in essence, to accept your employer's authority, even if you don't like it. In the second half, you are generally more flexible; it is easier to make legitimate choices about who and what will be an authority in your life. You will never live free of authority entirely, however — if God is in your box, you have automatically chosen to accept his authority.

The irony of the gospel, of course, is that the more you submit to the authority of Christ, the more radically free you become. This is what makes the second half so attractive to me. I see many young men and women in their twenties who are struggling hard to be free of their difficult jobs, tough marriages, and other externals that cannot be changed. I wouldn't want to live that way, and neither do they. When the discomfort level gets too high, they begin asking halftime questions. And once they figure out who's in the box, they realize they were struggling in vain. The way of the cross presents us with the greatest and most delicious paradox of all time: to be really free, you must submit to God's authority.

I hope that doesn't sound glib or overly "religious." I recognize the fact that even those who are sold out to Christ will face unfair bosses, dull jobs, kids who get in trouble, marriages that turn sour, and a whole host of life's problems. And I do not much care for the "just give it to the Lord" advice that is so easy to dispense. But I will say this: Once you have resolved your first-half issues and have decided that God is in your box, you will have more grace and freedom to live with those problems. They will not disappear — at least not instantly. But you will be in better shape to deal with them, to learn from them, even to turn them into opportunities for your life mission.

I was a committed Christian when I lost my son. I had already put God in the box and was beginning to implement a mission that made God the primary loyalty in my life. None of that prevented a horribly real external: raging currents can drown even the most powerful swimmer. It was hard enough to deal with that loss, but I can honestly say I do not think I would be where I am today had it not been for my faith. Respect the externals of the natural world and the authority of the supernatural world, and doing so will free you to grow and serve well in the second half.

CHAPTER 20

Playing for All You're Worth

So choose life in order that you may live ...
by loving the LORD your God, by obeying His voice,
and by holding fast to Him;
for this is your life and the length of your days.
Deuteronomy 30:19–20 NASB

Here is a secret you may not want to hear: getting from the first half to the second is not easy. It does not happen in a week, a month, a year. And the lines between the halves are not always clear.

Please don't let that hinder you from playing the game hard. It always occurs to me, when I share my story, that some could get the idea that all they have to do is follow a formula and things will turn out all right. Then, when the formula doesn't work, they get discouraged and resign themselves to the downward slope of their one curve. A good resource to keep you in the game is my book *Personal Coaching for Your Halftime Journey*, which is based on advice and encouragement I have shared over the years with people who are on the halftime journey.

I was in halftime for several transitional years, but I still played hard. And I had some fun along the way. You may make some false starts, need to go back and do some more seismic testing, or try another low-cost probe. As I've said before, the key is to start a new curve before the last one peters out.

A friend of mine has one foot in each of the "halfs." He's the managing partner of one of the largest real estate concerns in the world. When one of those cyclical downturns in the industry considerably reduced his net worth, he completely reorganized his company from an asset capital appreciation company to a service company. He has been developing new executives, and at the same time, he has a parallel career in a number of political and civic concerns — he is on the board of a college and is a very active teacher in his church. At some point he will make his parallel career his active one and turn his business over to someone else as I did. But not now. So he's in the first half, charging full-speed ahead to build his company; he's in halftime, taking stock of his life and deciding who's in the box; and he's in the second half, using his talents for a higher cause and working to reorder his life. He may be in all three places for a while longer, but he's playing hard and enjoying the game.

Remember, the second half is only part of the game. We all have to play the whole game.

I have been asked what sacrifices I have made in my life. That is a hard question to answer because I have most of the elements people seem to want — a vital marriage, lots of time to do with as I please, and financial security from the sale of a successful business. What I've had to give up to have those things is hours of "doing my own thing." Put another way, I have spent a good portion of my life on either side of the J-Zone in anxiety, waiting for a deal to go through, or in boredom, enduring the basics of business or of the spiritual disciplines.

I can't count the hours that I have spent reviewing corporate operations, giving managers their time to "show and tell," being an appropriate listener. And, of course, the best news to hear is always the least stimulating: "Everything's okay." I used to listen to Ross intently for fifteen minutes a day, using all the reflective listening techniques I could muster to stay on his train of thought. That may seem like a short time, but it seemed like an eternity when I arrived home with a jumble of "important" things on my mind and a need to relax and be apart from human conversation for a while.

Thomas Merton wrote that all you really need is in your life already. He called it the "hidden wholeness." What he meant was that you do not need to chase after things outside of you to find fulfillment. Even though that's what most of us do in the first half, we eventually learn that money, fame, material possessions, and experiences will never fill us. What we become in the second half has already been invested during the first; it is not going to come from out of the blue.

I used to think that if I ever said a complete yes to Christ, I would become a completely different person — that I would have to radically change my lifestyle to work full-time with AIDS sufferers in a third world country doing things I had never enjoyed doing. I am not denigrating those who have felt called and equipped for that type of mission, but am pointing out that they just weren't me. I couldn't figure out why God would equip me as an entrepreneur, conceiver, starter, team builder, manager, and leader and then put me someplace where those things cannot be fully integrated into my mission. I was relieved to discover that God does not waste what he has built. I am the same me as I was in the first half, only applied to a different venue. The same is true of you.

After God made you, he stepped back and said, "This is a great one!" He planted in your soul a desire to connect with him and then provided a way for you to do it. Whether you're in the first half of your life, in halftime, or playing the second half, God's desire is for you to serve him just by being who you are, by using what he gave you to work with.

CHAPTER 21

The Money Question

One of the most frequently asked questions about halftime has to do with money: do you have to be wealthy to have a significant second half? In fact, that question comes up so often I've included it in the Frequently Asked Questions section (see page 171). Because the "money issue" seems to be a barrier to so many, it deserves some additional thinking to clear up some misconceptions.

First, a simple answer: you do not have to be wealthy to enjoy a productive and significant second half. Halftime is not about money; it is about responding to your inner voice. People at all economic levels eventually sense the need to invest their lives in something more than their jobs, the pursuit of money or security, or whatever measure of success they might use. I believe it is a universal need that is placed within each of us, and regardless of your work situation or level of income, you can find ways to satisfy that longing to make a difference and leave a legacy. For example, Cathey Brown overcame various business struggles and her own alcoholism to start Rainbow Days, an agency that serves children of alcoholics. Lisa Trevino-Cummins got a job right out of college with Bank of America in Texas and convinced her employer to help redevelop inner-city neighborhoods. Ultimately, this led to her being tapped by President George W. Bush to lead his Faith-Based and Community Initiative. Talk about an exciting second-half mission from someone who was never wealthy! (See chapter 21 for more on the issue of halftime and wealth.)

It's true that people with significant wealth have more options and possibly more freedom to determine how they will invest themselves in the second half. When I made the decision to leave my first half, I knew that I could fund it with the capital I had accumulated. Not everyone can do that — in fact, probably the majority of people who read this book cannot. But I also know many wealthy people who "get" halftime but are waiting until they make just a little more money. They have allowed money to become an excuse for business as usual. At the same time, I know people who depend on a regular paycheck to pay the mortgage and other living expenses but are having the times of their lives pursuing adventures that exploit all their gifts and abilities for a greater good.

Another popular misconception that goes along with the "only wealthy people can do it" argument is the idea that halftime is really just an early retirement with a new hobby. In other words, wealthy people have the luxury to "quit work," enjoy life, and write checks to a favorite charity or volunteer occasionally with a nonprofit.

Halftime is actually the opposite of retirement, an alternative to the boredom most retirees experience. In reality, you may work harder in your second half than you did in the first. I know I have. When I handed the operating leadership of my company over to someone else so that I could devote my primary energy to my second-half mission, my work schedule did not change appreciably. I still went to my office every day, sat through long meetings, hired people, brokered deals, and traveled.

We have to be careful with the idea that the object of work is to earn enough money so that we can someday quit working and live a life of leisure. As the late Fred Smith Sr. once told me, "Work is the psychological glue that holds a person together." There's a fascinating study in the book *Flow* by Mihály Csíkszentmihályi in which the author attached beepers to individuals and polled their levels of satisfaction at different times. Although they all expressed a desire for more leisure time, they actually expressed much higher levels of satisfaction while they were working in pursuit of some meaningful goal than when they were engaged in sedentary activity. Leisure is an occasional gift we need to give ourselves regardless of our life stage, but full-time leisure, as appealing as it may sound, is simply not good for your mental or emotional health. It never works.

If your motivation for halftime is leisure or more free time, then maybe you just need a long vacation or a sabbatical. It is not unusual for people in stressful jobs to run out of steam and take an extended break, but that shouldn't be confused with halftime. Halftime is more about time and talent than it is about treasure. It starts with the question, "What do I believe?" and moves to "What do I do with what I believe?" It is about taking your God-given talents and all that you have learned in your first-half career and finding ways to use those for the greater good. Few people are able to connect their work to their beliefs in the first half. The second half gives everyone a greater opportunity to do that.

Halftime Mission, Full-Time Job

So how do you experience a fulfilling halftime if you don't have several million dollars in the bank? How do you pursue a second-half mission if you need a regular paycheck? You follow the same process described in this book. Listen to the still, small voice. Locate your mainstream, identifying your "one thing" to put in the box. Spend some time taking stock of what you have to offer in terms of skills, knowledge, and gifts. Explore opportunities to align your passion with others' needs. You don't need a penny to do this — just a commitment to listen, study, and explore.

Once you have a fairly clear idea of what you feel called to do, how your skills and knowledge can be invested in a greater cause — the *what* — begin looking for ways to do it — the *how* — and here's where you have a distinct advantage over previous generations. Prior to the 1970s, people approaching middle age really didn't have the options you have. If you were a bank manager, you probably stayed with your bank until retirement; and if you made it to sixty-five, you were too tired to do much more than enjoy your grandchildren. Besides, you did not have that many productive years left, due to a life expectancy that was significantly shorter than it is now. As Peter Drucker pointed out in the foreword to this book, in 1929 the average life expectancy in the United States was not even fifty years. Even if you feel you cannot pursue halftime until you retire, you will still have anywhere from ten to twenty years of a reasonably healthy and active life ahead of you. But don't wait until retirement. Here are just a few strategies for getting started right away:

Know your financial position. While it is true that halftime involves some level of financial commitment, you may be in better financial shape than you think. When most people approach middle age, their financial needs begin to decline. Mortgages are either paid off or close to being paid off. The kids are out on their own, which means lower grocery bills, fewer trips to clothing and shoe stores, less of your paycheck being set aside for college funds. And if you were wise enough to contribute to a savings accounts or mutual fund, you probably have at least a small nest egg that could help provide seed capital for a second-half enterprise. Then again, college and weddings, along with a few other unplanned emergencies may have left you little or no extra funds, which will affect how you implement halftime. Knowledge is power, and once you know where you stand financially, you will be able to scale your second-half plans accordingly.

Find or start a mission you can afford. While there will always be some risk involved in halftime, which I'll address later, no one should irresponsibly jump in over his head in pursuit of his half-time dream. Ideally, whatever you choose to do should be sustainable, since you won't have a lasting impact if your endeavor bankrupts you. When I began Leadership Network, my primary second-half platform twenty-five years ago, we began with what we then called "two guys and a typewriter." Now there are fifty employees and a whole web of collaborative organizations and contractors. I made sure I had enough money to keep my mission alive for the long haul. Again, halftime isn't about money — it's about mission, and once you discover yours, you will find a way to carry it out responsibly. Money follows good ideas.

For example, I know of a doctor who, although he earned a comfortable salary, decided he could live on less so that he could invest his time and talent in his mission. He did not sacrifice his well-earned vacations but instead took additional time off his practice to go on missions of mercy, providing medical treatment to remote villages in the developing world. He earned less money, because when you don't see patients, you don't get paid. And he also paid for the medical supplies out of his own funds. I don't know his financial situation, but my guess is that his lifestyle didn't change much. The kind of sacrifice most upper-middle-class individuals might make is trading a Lexus for a Buick, or investing slightly less in a mutual fund. The doctor's second-half plan was affordable yet highly significant, as he had the satisfaction of knowing that entire villages were healthier because of him.

Small business owner Bob Lee began his second half close to retirement age and now spends considerable time each year riding a bicycle thousands of miles across the United States to raise money for three charities, thus the name of his second-half mission: A Ride for Three Reasons (*www.3reasons.org*). While Lee never had the multimillion-dollar nest egg to finance his second half, he managed his money well so that he would be able to pursue significance without causing his family to starve. He knew he wouldn't be able to live off his retirement, so he set aside money in a savings account over the years. As he entered his sixties, he had this hollow feeling, inherently knowing retirement clearly wasn't the best option for him. He had enjoyed success in his career and now wanted significance.

Knowing that drawing from his savings and retirement wouldn't be enough, Lee embarked on a "parallel career," starting a small window-covering business that provides both the extra income and the freedom to take several weeks off for his bike trips. He still needs to work, but in addition to enjoying his passion for cycling, he receives great satisfaction in knowing that he is helping people who benefit from the charities he supports.

Renegotiate your work situation. The difficulty in finding skilled replacement employees and the rising costs of recruiting and training those replacements has lead many employers to do whatever is reasonable to keep their experienced workers. Therefore, if you are a valuable employee, you have an unprecedented opportunity to bargain with your employer for a work situation that allows you to invest in the second half. Options that employers may offer include reducing your workload/workweek (with or without reducing your pay), granting additional time off beyond earned vacation time, allowing company time and resources for nonprofit work, and providing sabbaticals. Dennis Reynolds works full-time as comptroller of my Leadership Network organization but has an arrangement with us that allows him to work for legendary social entrepreneur Tillie Burgin at Mission Arlington, which serves the homeless.

Downsize yourself. One of the interesting outcomes of corporate downsizing is the number of people who lost their jobs and either started their own small businesses or became "contract" workers, often ending up better off financially than when they worked for their company. Michael Williams found himself on the short end of a downsizing strategy, but as a contract worker serving his former employer plus a dozen other businesses, he is actually making more money than ever. He says, "Now I get to call my own shots and can take time off whenever I want to pursue the thing I am most passionate about." He lost his job, but he couldn't stop working because he still had to make his house payment and support his family. But as a contract worker, he is less tied to corporate schedules and policies that kept him from being able to pursue his dream.

Simplify your work. Ryan Daniels was an account executive for a major advertising agency, and by the time he was forty, he had a very high-paying job that demanded seventy-hour weeks with a bonus of unrelenting stress. He heard that inner voice telling him he couldn't keep living like that. Yet he still needed a job. He moved to a much smaller company where he could, in his own words, "coast" and still excel. In essence, he gave himself an additional twenty to thirty hours a week, which he used to mentor less-experienced marketing professionals in nonprofit ministries. Ask yourself, "Is all this stress and long hours worth the big paycheck?" If not, you could either do what Ryan did or hire on directly with a nonprofit and let your full-time job also become your second-half career.

Risk and Rewards

I do not want to imply that entering halftime when you need your weekly paycheck is without risks. I know it may seem scarier for you than for me to make a significant shift in your career, but nothing of value is without risk.

Every person alive has what the famed Swiss psychologist Carl Jung called a "life task" encoded within his or her being. The Greeks called it "destiny." The Bible says that God has a set of works "prepared beforehand" for us to do. If we don't finally get around to actualizing this unique calling, it follows us around the rest of our lives like an accusing shadow.

This is the hero's journey. And it is not just reserved for Bill Gates and Warren Buffet. Think of Wendy Kopp, who as a Princeton senior with, I expect, meager funds, formed Teach for America to encourage elite college graduates to spend their first two years teaching in inner-city schools. More than seventeen thousand top students have followed her lead so far, and there's a huge waiting list of students who want to follow their lead.

We have all heard that people do not live on bread alone. Regardless of your financial condition, as you approach midlife, you will likely begin to get restless with your current work. Pay attention to that restlessness, because it is the yearning of your soul to become what you were divinely wired to be. You can dampen that yearning with plenty of excuses, and money is often the biggest reason for ignoring that still, small voice. The riches you will gain for obeying the call to significance will outweigh any financial loss you think you will experience if you pursue your halftime dream.

CHAPTER 22

A 50/50 Proposition

I began this book with my epitaph: 100X. It expresses my desire to be remembered as one who greatly multiplied the seed planted in me by my heavenly Father.

I would like to close with another mathematical formula: 50/50. It expresses my dream for everyone who is en route to the second half.

Several years ago, Sandy Kress, a Jewish lawyer, and Don Williams, a Christian businessman, put their heads together to find ways to improve the Dallas public school system. The schools had been working with test scores, hiring practices, and other technical matters and had seen some improvements. The missing piece of the puzzle was the morals and values dimension. I was part of a diverse, multisector, multicultural group selected by Sandy and Don to wrestle with this thorny issue. Ultimately, we centered our efforts on six different initiatives, one of which was the "50/50 church."

The basic idea of the 50/50 church has been to challenge Dallas churches to allocate 50 percent of their resources to themselves and 50 percent to serving their community and world. This may sound like a simple enough idea, but in terms of individuals and churches, it's radical. Most churches feel they are stretching themselves if they spend a tenth of their time, talents, energy, and money on ministry beyond their own congregations. Think of what could happen in your community if every church adopted this 50/50 formula! And think of what would happen to you if you spent half of your time and resources on yourself and your family and the other half on others.

One of the central changes that makes the second half different from the first half is that in the second half the life of faith becomes much more integrated instead of segregated. In second-half living, you will learn that the principle of altruistic egoism is true: doing good to others does just as much good for you. Your life will be a balanced living-out of the gospel, a winsome, attractive, and joyful witness to the fact that life in Christ adds rather than detracts, fills rather than empties. You will have a difficult time marking the boundary between self and others, because significance has overshadowed success. Instead of trying to manage the various compartments of your life, you will be your whole self and take great pleasure in all that entails.

Just take a look at the following list of opposing values and attitudes and ask yourself, "Which side do I want to be on during the second half of my life?"

Segregated Life	Integrated Life
Personal, private faith	Ministry as part of life
Dogmatism	Paradox
What to believe	What to do about what I believe
Faith means giving up	Faith means addition, abundance, wholeness
We/They:	Us:
That which separates us	That which draws us together
We/They, cont.:	Us, cont.:
Individual sport	Team sport
Independence	Interdependence
Law	Grace
Obligation	Personal choices

Segregated Life	Integrated Life
External approach	Internal approach
Based on appearances	"As a man thinketh, so is he"
Authoritarian leadership	Servant leader
Sunday Christianity	Seven-day-a-week Christianity
Doctrine-driven	Purpose-driven

The 50/50 church will depend on individuals embracing these new values in order to serve its surrounding community, living out its proclamation of the gospel rather than imposing an unwelcome ideology on others. Its witness is first by example, then by proclamation. The role of the 50/50 church is to place carriers of faith back into all of the contradictions, tensions, and paradoxes of the community, rather than to isolate people in an unrealistic, cloistered atmosphere for a couple of hours on Sunday morning.

I know I am not the first person to suggest that the church needs to do a better job of interacting with the world. Every believer, I am certain, wrestles with this and truly wants to see the gospel transform our culture. So why doesn't it happen?

I believe the answer lies in individual responsibility. The church will never have credibility in the community at large without *expressed* individual responsibility. People need to *see* our faith, not merely hear about it. When our beliefs are personal and privatized, practiced only inside a building one day a week, we Christians miss out on that glorious opportunity to be salt and light. Worse, I believe that when faith continues to be directed inward, we become one-dimensional, uninteresting, and wholly self-centered persons. We have a work life, a family life, a community life, and a church life. And when segregated like that, each sphere is less robust than it could be.

What does this have to do with your second half? One of the real tragedies of the first half is that people are encouraged to be selfish. No one really wants to put career ahead of family, but it happens — the inertia of trying to be successful is just too great for most of us to resist. The third decade of most everyone's life is practically a blur, with little time to think through any of the core issues and values that lead to significance. I do not know if this is inevitable; I just know that it happens a lot, and that it almost always culminates in a period of questioning and self-doubt. *Is this all there is?* we wonder. *Do I want to do this for the rest of my life?*

Eventually, your first half will end. The clock will run out. If it happens unexpectedly — if you do not take responsibility for going into halftime and ordering your life so that your second half is better than the first, you will join the ranks of those who are coasting their way to retirement. Your second half will be a slower version of the first, with fewer and fewer successes and very little significance. But if you take responsibility for the way you play out the rest of the game, you will begin to experience the abundant life our Lord intended for you.

When I look across the Christian landscape in America, I see a powerful reservoir of energy just waiting to be unleashed. I see enough talent, creativity, compassion, money, and strength to transform our culture. I see true believers in every sector of society genuinely concerned about the condition of their communities but feeling powerless to do something significant to change it.

My life mission, to somehow transform that latent energy in American Christianity to active energy, may seem impossible, but as a bona fide second-halfer, I don't think in terms of the impossible anymore. I honestly believe that I can play a role in releasing the tremendous energy lying dormant in the church — but I also know that I cannot do it alone.

At one point in my halftime, I thought of myself as an arsonist — someone who likes to light fires in people, then sit back and watch them blaze. But the metaphor is not entirely accurate, because I really don't like to just sit back and watch. Still, I do like to light fires in people, and I hope I've ignited something within you, for I believe in every Christian's heart a spark is glowing.

And I hope you are feeling the heat of that spark, and that you are growing wonderfully uncomfortable with it.

I hope that when you consider your second half, you begin to feel a breeze blowing deep within, that you begin to see what kind of fire you might become.

I hope that as that spark begins to ignite, you get excited, animated; that you start to feel young again; that you begin to dream new dreams.

I hope that as the flames spread, you realize you can't smother the fire this time; that this is not the puff of good intentions, but a hurricane of commitment.

That is the energy I see when I look into the sanctuaries, Sunday school classrooms, and Bible studies of America's churches. That's the kind of energy I know is within you.

I have concluded that individual responsibility is the key to transforming the church. I can describe for you an effective and feasible program that will position you for significance, but in the final analysis, you alone must choose how you want to live. You have the freedom to decide whether you want the rest of your years to be the *best* of your years.

My prayer for you is that you will have the courage to live the dreams that God has placed within you.

See you at the end of the game.

www.halftime.org/nextsteps

Frequently Asked Questions

Hardly a day goes by that I don't get a letter or an email from someone asking questions about halftime. Following are some of the most frequently asked questions. I have also written a book titled *Beyond Halftime* that addresses questions people have asked me regarding halftime.

Q *Do I need to quit my job in order to have the kind of second half you describe?*

No, but you may need to renegotiate how you work. For example, many successful second-halfers who are still with their first-half employer have negotiated their commitment to half- or three-quarter time. Or, let's say you love your job and you need its income, but you want to invest yourself into something with more significance. Many employers have become increasingly generous in allowing leave time for their employees to pursue activities that give back to the community.

Q *Do you have to be wealthy to have a successful second half?*

Absolutely not. I know many people who have not enjoyed significant wealth but have made the transition from success to significance. Think of the parable of the talents (Matthew 25:14–30), in which each of three servants was given an assignment according to his own ability. The servant who multiplied two talents — a monetary unit — was honored as much as the servant who multiplied five talents. When you come to the end of your time here on earth, you will not be judged for what you had but by what you did with what you had. Relatively few people can quit their jobs for second-half work, but many teachers, lawyers, middle managers, and sales professionals are able to adjust their work requirements so that they can invest themselves in a second half just as invigorating and helpful to others as the contributions of those who have greater financial resources.

Q *I'm in my late fifties. Is it too late to enter halftime?*

It's never too late to shift your emphasis from getting ahead to contributing to others. I know people who are in their sixties who have decided to change and realize they could have twenty years of second-half significance. Most people miss the second half because they plan on doing it "someday." Someday is either right now or never. With life-expectancy growing and earlier retirement ages, the majority of the new halftimers could be retirees.

Q *Is halftime only for men?*

That's a great question, one I've thought a lot about since I first wrote *Halftime*. On the one hand, most of the people I know who have entered the second half are men. Part of the reason for that may be that for my generation, a lot of women chose to stay home with their children. Yet women are just as hungry for significance as men. Everything I've written about halftime will apply to women who enter the professional world right out of college. Women who have spent fifteen to twenty years caring for their families may rightly believe they are doing truly significant work and now want to enter the professional world. Halftime is not really a gender issue as much as a "life circumstance" issue.

Q *I was just beginning to look forward to retirement. What's wrong with taking it easy after putting in so many years of hard work?*

Nothing, and if you've worked at your career for twenty-five to thirty years, you may indeed need some time off. But I can almost guarantee that within two years you'll be bored. Instead of becoming a greeter at a discount store, use all the skills you developed in your career and find a way to use them to help others. And use that time off as halftime — finding your "one thing" and exploring ways to build a mission around it.

Q *Is halftime always preceded by a crisis?*

Not always, though often a major event in our lives gets our attention and starts us thinking about what really matters. In my case, I think I would have still entered halftime had I not lost my son. His death may have accelerated a process that had already begun. By the time most people are fifty, they have taken at least one pretty big hit below the waterline — a divorce, death of a loved one, loss of a job, or a health crisis such as a heart attack. But even without these things, it is natural for people in their fourth decade to begin examining their lives more deeply.

Q *What if I launch out in a second-half adventure and discover it's not working or it isn't really for me after all? Can I change directions?*

Certainly. In fact, you may have one or more "false starts" that don't quite work out. The beauty of the second half is that you really do get to call the shots. Keep in mind, however, that your projects may change but your mission should remain constant. That's why it's so important to spend enough time in halftime settling the question, "What am I here for?"

Q *You seem so passionate about helping others. I don't feel that way. When I think about the second half, I want to do something for me. Am I just selfish?*

Not really. Doing something for yourself and doing something for others are not opposite ends of a continuum. The whole point of altruistic egoism is that when you help others, you help yourself even more. The opposite is also true: if you focus solely on yourself, you will eventually become restless, even miserable. Start with the questions, "What do I want to do?" and "What makes me really happy?" Then find ways to do those things in a way that helps others. For example, if you love sports, trying to find significance by serving food in a soup kitchen will not bring as much fulfillment as volunteering to coach an inner-city Little League team. God wired you the way he did for a purpose.

Q *I'm already so busy doing things for others — I serve on my church board and school board, I teach a Sunday school class, and I volunteer at the community food pantry. I can't imagine leaving any of those activities without disappointing people.*

First, you can't let the prospect of disappointing people rule your life. But one of the humbling truths I have learned is that I'm not indispensable. After you leave a board, someone will come along who can do the job as well or better than you did. Second, ultimately you will do more good if you have more time to focus on your own agenda.

Q *Is halftime only for Christians or people who have a religious faith?*

No. Anyone can experience significance by using their skills and knowledge to help others. Even though my personal mission is to release the latent energy of large Christian churches, I could just as easily be investing my second half in trying to help develop entrepreneurs in under-resourced countries. It all goes back to the question I raised in chapter 5: What's in the box? Once you locate the mainspring of your life, you will find ways to let that identify your second-half mission.

Questions for Reflection and Discussion

Introduction: Opening the Heart's Holiest Chamber

1. No one in the middle of life likes to think about the finish line, but doing so can have a profound impact on how well you live. So take a few minutes to consider the end of your life. How do you want other people to remember you? What legacy would you like to leave?

2. Reflect on the first half of your life. Rank the following in terms of how they dominated your time and resources: education, advancement of a career, family, acquiring possessions (home, cars, toys, etc.).

3. Do you ever have thoughts that the clock of your life is ticking and that there are things you want to accomplish that you haven't had time to do? What are some of those things, and what has prevented you from doing them?

Chapter 1: Listening to the Gentle Whisper

1. When you think about your life right now, what are some adjectives or descriptive phrases that come to mind (e.g., *excitement, passion, in a rut, bored*)?

2. Review the diagram on page 33. Where are you on the bases? How long have you been there? On a scale of 1 to 10 (with 1

being low and 10 being high), how motivated are you to move to the next base?

3. How is your behavior influenced by your faith? Is it primarily through the things you don't do because of your faith or the things that you do? Is there anything you would like to change about that? If so, what?

4. What are one or two of the big successes of your first half? What makes them so satisfying to you?

5. In addition to your family, what are you most passionate about (e.g., the environment, adoption, education, poverty)? How could you gain further clarity about your passion?

6. If it were two years from now and you were living the perfect second half, how would you know?

Halftime Assignment #1: Reading Your Story

To help you see how everything you have done in your first half sets up the rest of the story — how your first half is preparation for a better second half — reflect on the following questions:

- If your story up until now was going to be published in book form, what would its title be?

- If your story was a movie, who would play your role? Why?

- If your story built up to a major achievement you have made, what would that be? Why were you able to reach that achievement?

- If your story was an epic, what noble cause have you been championing? What was the motivation behind your accomplishments?

- Describe a scene in your story in which you faced a major setback that brought out the best in you. What characteristic or personal quality did this reveal?

- What other setbacks did you face, and what did you learn from them?

- What events in your story foreshadow what lies ahead for you? What parts of your story do you want to leave out in the second half of your life? What parts do you want to include? What remains to be done?

- Who have been the most important people in your story thus far, and what role will they play in the rest of your story?

Now that you have thought about how your first half will be a springboard for the second half, list several bullet points for how you would like the rest of your story to read. One technique to help you identify these points is to ask yourself, "What things do I want to accomplish with my life before I am unwilling or unable to contribute any more?"

Below are some examples to jump-start your thinking.

During my second half I want to:

- negotiate a gradual reduction in my commitments at work so that by age fifty I will be doing "paid" work no more than twenty-four hours per week

- build a trusted team of three advisers with whom I can share my halftime dream and my second-half journey

- send a letter of introduction to ten nonprofit leaders whose work I resonate with, offering to buy lunch and talk about whether there's a role for me in their organization

- develop partnerships with software and hardware providers

- raise capital

- launch a pro bono on-site computer training program to overseas missionaries

- take a "vision trip" to another country ... or to another side of town

Now use these bullet points as a "cheat sheet" and tell your second-half story into a voice recorder. Play it back and begin thinking about how you can turn this story into your second half.

Chapter 2: The Hour of Reverse Conversion

1. When you were in high school, what did you dream of becoming as an adult? Is that what you are doing today? If not, what changed your plans?

2. What gifts or talents make you a good fit for your work?

3. In addition to your work, how could those gifts or talents be used more fully to serve God and others?

4. What have been the major turning points in your life? Which events have shaped your career? Your family life? Your social life? Your spiritual life?

5. In what way are you currently at a turning point in your life? What influences or events are leading you to think a new direction or a change is in order?

Chapter 3: A Season of Searching and Self-Help

1. Bob Buford writes that "a company, just like a person, needs to periodically shift its focus in order to achieve healthy growth" (page 47). How have you personally shifted your focus in the past decade?

2. Bob writes about a question that tugged at his mind: "What will I lose with all this gaining?" How would you answer that in your own career? What have you lost as you have gained success in your career?

3. In any given week, what percentage of your time and energy is devoted to your work? Your family? Your church or faith community? Your community?

4. If over the next two to five years you could change any of those percentages, how would they change and why?

5. From an even bigger picture perspective, list three to five things you most want to accomplish in life (see author's list on page 49). Imagine the types of things you may need to do to make sure you accomplish them.

Chapter 4: Success Panic

1. In the opening pages of this chapter, Bob describes a quiet intruder that disturbed his life at age forty-four — success panic. Have you hit a threshold where you wondered, *How much is enough?* When did this happen, and what are your thoughts as you have reflected on that question?

2. Have you ever had thoughts of leaving your career to do something completely different? If so, what led you to those thoughts?

3. What aspects of your work bring you the greatest joy? What aspects bring you the greatest annoyances or stresses? Which of these two polarities gets most of your attention?

4. In your current work, do you feel driven or called? Explain.

5. Make a continuum by drawing a line across a piece of paper. On one end of the line write "Success," and on the other, "Significance." Pinpoint where you are on this continuum and make a note of today's date. Are you satisfied with where you are? Why or why not?

Chapter 5: Locating the Mainspring

1. What "dreams" did you have in your first half that are still beckoning? Are new dreams emerging?

2. List two or three things you are really good at (e.g., analyzing statistics, managing people, creating systems). What steps could you take to refine your understanding of your unique abilities?

3. How could your unique talents figure into your halftime plan?

4. In what ways might your job align with your dreams and ultimately your legacy? In what ways could it get in the way of them?

5. In what ways might your life need to change if you were to focus 80 percent of your time and energy on the one thing about which you are most passionate?

6. Bob writes, "It follows the same wonderfully inverted logic as the ancient assertion that it is in giving that one receives, in our weakness we are made strong, and in dying we are born to a richer life." In what ways have you experienced this paradox of following Christ wholeheartedly?

Chapter 6: "Adios, Ross"

1. What are some areas of your life or experiences you have had where you had absolutely no control over the outcome? What events have "shaken you out of your comfort zone"?

2. What did you learn about yourself as you went through those experiences? About God?

3. Bob says that "utter emptiness and brokenness left me feeling awful and wonderful at the same time." What do you think he

meant? Can you think of anything in your own life that left you feeling the same way?

4. In this chapter Bob describes a simple Quaker prayer that begins by praying with palms upward to visualize all that you need from God, and then praying with palms downward to visualize leaving your cares in God's capable hands. What do you need from God, and what cares do you want to leave in his hands?

5. What is your "eternal perspective" — based on Romans 8:28 — and how is it played out in your day-to-day life? How does the hope of eternal life affect the way you live in the here and now?

Chapter 7: Taking Stock

1. As you have worked through these important second-half issues, how much time have you been able to carve out to spend reflecting on the "bigger picture" of your life? (Think hours per week.) Do you ever wish you had more time for such reflection? Why or why not?

2. Here's a bold step: take out your calendar and block out a half hour per day for the next two weeks that you will devote to thinking about the direction your life is heading and changes that you would like to make. In the last half hour slot, insert a note to ask yourself what the two or three most important things were that came out of that "think time."

3. Bob writes about dealing with our regrets of the past by accepting them as valuable learning experiences instead of beating ourselves up about them. What are some of your regrets, and what have you learned from them that you can apply to the future?

Halftime Assignment #2: Know Your Strengths

An important part of taking stock is to assess your current arsenal of skills. Use some of your reflection time to fill out the following, and ask a few close friends for their comments and perspectives on your strengths:

current job/position/roles

key responsibilities

abilities required (see list below)

abilities (use list from pages 69–70 of *Game Plan* by Bob Buford [Grand Rapids, Mich.: Zondervan, 1998])

Now go back to the "key responsibilities" and place each of them in one of the following quadrants. Do the same for "abilities required."

High Ability/ High Satisfaction	Low Ability/ High Satisfaction
• developing new talent • counseling • mentoring	• long-range planning • prescribing • imagining
High Ability/ Low Satisfaction	**Low Ability/ Low Satisfaction**
• overseeing $100 million budget • analyzing • formulating	• managing junior staff • directing

The object of this assignment is to help you begin to focus on the areas that will give you the highest return for your physical and emotional energy. Ideally, your second half will find you spending most of your time in the upper left quadrant.

Chapter 8: What Do You Believe?

1. Bob writes about understanding God and knowing God. What is the difference? Which do you think is more important and why?

2. Describe your relationship with God as honestly as possible. What do you understand about God? How well do you *know* God? What are your doubts about God? What are you doing to know God better?

3. How satisfied are you with the way your faith is integrated into the rest of your life? What is preventing you from integrating your faith more fully into the rest of your life?

4. What is the most noticeable way in which your faith and your work life connect? Your faith and your marriage? Your faith and your family? Your faith and your community? Your faith and your service?

5. Halftime is not a Christian phenomenon, but when we reflect on significance, it often begs answers to spiritual questions. What spiritual questions do you need answers to when you think about making a lasting impact in this world?

Chapter 9: Finding Your One Thing

1. Bob says that most people in the first half try to fill a void in their lives by materialism (making and spending money/ acquiring things), competition (winning, accomplishing big things), or relationships. Which of these is most likely to clutter your thinking as you try to find your one primary second-half focus?

2. What are you doing now that you love so much — that gives you so much satisfaction — that you would do it without pay? What do you find so fulfilling about it?

3. Have you pursued dreams and desires of other people for your life instead of your own dreams and desires? List two or three examples from your past.

4. What do you feel is the primary loyalty of your life that should go in your "box"?

5. Review last week's calendar. What percentage of your appointments align with your deepest passion and core values? What does this tell you about your life? Do you believe it is possible to align your life more fully with your deepest passion and core values? Why or why not?

Halftime Assignment #3: What's in Your Box?

Look over the following list, and in the space provided, write down at least one thing you have sacrificed in order to develop or care for the individual, things, or activities listed:

spouse	car
children	sports/exercise
career	community service
health	politics
hobbies or personal interests	church
house	religious beliefs
vacation	addictions
education	other

Now go back over this list and try to isolate two or three categories that stand out as being the most important to you. Which ones would you not be willing to give up?

I suspect that you have narrowed your three down to these general areas: family, religious belief, career. To get an honest picture of your allegiance, however, I would urge you to drill down on the career side. What is it specifically about your career that motivates you? In my case it wasn't so much that I liked running a cable television company. I liked managing things so that my business would prosper, and the way to measure how well I managed was the bottom line. Therefore, one of the things competing for the box for me was money, symbolized by the dollar sign.

Narrowing down your loyalties to two or three as you did above helps you see your areas of priority, but it isn't enough for a second-half game plan. Eventually you must choose one, or else your second half will be pretty much a repeat of the first. You will be easily influenced by other agendas because you have not established your own "one thing." Select a symbol for each of the three things you listed and place them inside the circles below:

Your goal is to choose one of these symbols and put it in the box, but don't do it right now. Take some time. Involve your spouse and perhaps one or two trusted friends. Spend some time by yourself, praying and meditating and trying to listen to that still, small voice.

Chapter 10: From Success to Significance

1. How have you measured success in your career so far? On a scale of 1 to 10, with 10 being highly successful, where do you rate yourself?

2. What discoveries in your life signaled to you that success wasn't enough?

3. How would you define the difference between success and significance?

4. Bob writes of "reordering our personal myth" (page 90). What is your personal myth, and how would you reorder it if you could?

5. To bring even more clarity about what you feel is significance, craft the perfect job for yourself — perhaps in the marketplace or ministry or nonprofit — one that would fully use your talents to benefit others.

Chapter 11: Finding the Center and Staying There

1. Do you agree with Bob that most of our time in the first half of our careers is spent between anxiety and boredom? Why or why not? Is this true for you?

2. Review the list of seven tensions on page 93. Do you ever feel caught between these extremes? In what ways? Can you give an example?

3. Bob writes about the "zone" — that moment in time and space when the tensions of winning and losing, physics and the supernatural, human and spirit, are suspended ever so briefly. Have you ever been in the zone? Describe what it was like and what you think caused it. How are you learning to deal with — and thrive among — these tensions?

4. Have you ever accepted a great assignment or opportunity that just didn't feel as if it fit you but you knew you could be successful at it? How did it turn out? How did you feel when you completed the assignment?

5. In the Bible, Jesus was tempted in the desert by three powerful forces:

• material works and needs (turn the stones into bread)

• fame (jump off the top of the temple without harming himself)

• power (own all the kingdoms of the world)

Perhaps we all face these forces. Which of these three would have the greatest pull on you? Why? What has been most helpful to you in resisting this temptation?

Chapter 12: Staying in the Game but Adjusting the Plan

1. Most people in halftime cannot just leave their work. So, as you begin considering possible second-half opportunities, spend some time thinking realistically about how they would be funded. Will you be able to leave your job and live off your savings? Will you need to keep your current job? Is it possible to renegotiate your current relationship with your employer? What about a paying job in a nonprofit? Which of these options fit your situation the best?

2. What is your attitude toward your job? Attitudes can range from "I love my job so much, I'd do it even if they didn't pay me" to "I can't stand what I do no matter how much money I make." Draw a line on a piece of paper showing these two extremes. Mark an X to show where your attitude is toward your work.

3. What does Bob mean by "seismic testing" as it relates to halftime, and how would you conduct your own seismic testing? Be specific.

4. In what ways could you create some margin in your career so that you can infuse significance into your life without selling your company or bailing from corporate America?

5. With a little realignment, many halftimers find that their current career is a platform for significance. What are some specific things you could do in your job that could be seen as your higher calling or mission?

6. Would you be willing to reduce your income by 20 percent to have more time and freedom to pursue your second-half mission? Why or why not? How could you actually do that with your current job? With a different job?

Chapter 13: Overlapping Curves

1. On the Sigmoid Curve below, write the letter *A* on the spot where you think you are. If you are on the upward slope of the curve, what steps will you take to start a new curve? If you are on the downward slope, what are some things you can do to regain energy, vision, and momentum?

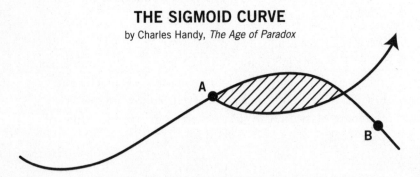

THE SIGMOID CURVE
by Charles Handy, *The Age of Paradox*

A

B

2. Starting the next curve early has proven to be wise, but it is not easy. An important first step is to identify two or three uncertainties that could keep you from making a concrete move into a second-half mission.

3. What can you do to overcome the fear that those uncertainties (above) create?

4. Bob says that too many people wait until they are finished with their current project or career before they plan to embark on something new. Realistically, when will you be finished with what you are doing? Are you willing to wait that long to start something new? How will the benefits of waiting outweigh the risks of the uncertainties of starting now?

5. More than ever before, people are taking early retirement. What impact will retirement have on your second-half career? How can you avoid the fate Peter Drucker describes: "Retirees have not proved to be the fertile source of volunteer effort we once thought they would be. They cut their engines off and lose their edge." What would have to happen in your life for you to be fully engaged in a "parallel career" within the next ten years? If you are interested in a parallel career, list specific steps necessary and a date for completing each step.

Chapter 14: Leaping into the Abyss

1. While the first half is usually all about gaining, which sometimes results in loss, the second half is more about releasing and relinquishing, which usually results in redirection. List three to five things you will have to release or relinquish to move into your second half. How might that result in gaining?

2. By now you should have some ideas about what you would like to do in your second half. List as many as come to mind, even in the most general terms, in the space below (e.g., do something involving inner-city kids and literacy, find a way to use my operational skills for a nonprofit, do something involving travel overseas, form a foundation to invest in other people's ministries).

3. Now go back over that list. Describe one exploratory experience you could seek with each idea as well as a date when you hope to complete that exploratory experience.

4. Consider inviting your spouse on a getaway weekend to talk about your second half. Begin your time by asking about your spouse's dreams and what you can do to help your spouse live them out. Then ask if you can go over this list together and get your spouse's insights about what fits you best.

5. As you begin to pursue your second-half dreams, it is very important that you share them with others around you to gain their insights. Who are some other people you need to share your dream with, and when will you do it (e.g., friends, employer, pastor, children, et al.)?

Chapter 15: Life Mission

1. What is the mission statement of the organization you work for? How does it guide you in your particular role? How much time do the leaders of your organization devote to keeping the mission statement in front of the entire organization?

2. A mission provides important focus not only for organizations but for individuals. Based on what you know about your strengths, passions, core beliefs, and values, what words or concepts come to mind when you think of your life's mission?

3. On page 120 Bob details a number of life commitments. What are your commitments in life? List seven different areas, using this list as a catalyst for your own ideas.

4. Bob says that his personal mission statement released him to be himself. What are some aspects of your personality, your beliefs, your values, and your dreams that you would like to be released?

5. Peter Drucker offered two basic questions to help you discover the unique role God has prepared for you: What have you achieved? What do you care deeply about? How would you answer each question?

Halftime Assignment #4:
Write Your Personal Mission Statement

To help you begin writing your personal mission statement, answer the following questions. (Going back and considering your answers to some of the Questions for Reflection and Discussion from previous chapters may be helpful.)

1. What do I believe?

2. What do I do uncommonly well?

3. What is my passion?

4. What needs exist in the world that I would like to meet? What do I bring to the party that others need and could benefit from?

5. What are the "should haves" that have trailed me all through the first half that I really care about?

6. How could my story and God's larger story connect?

7. What difference do I want to make through my efforts?

On a plain sheet of paper, try to capture your personal mission in one hundred words. When you are finished, critique it with these questions:

1. Is it clear?
2. Does it support what's in the box?
3. Is it big enough? If I could create those results, would it be worth living for?
4. Is it action-oriented?
5. Does it express a deeply held passion in my life?
6. Does it allow me to share myself?
7. Is it true to my authentic or truest self?

Now spend some time to try and reduce this larger statement into a sentence or two that could fit on a T-shirt.

Chapter 16: Regaining Control

1. Do you ever feel as if you have way too much to do? In what ways is your life overflowing with good things that may be the enemy of the very best?

2. Psychologist Mihály Csíkszentmihályi says, "People who control inner experience will be able to determine the quality of their lives." What inner experiences can you control?

3. Are your possessions draining you physically, financially, or emotionally? How could you downsize to regain some control of your life and resources? What are your biggest "hesitancies" to reducing your possessions?

4. The Halftime ministry team has developed an online tool to declutter your time and create some space and capacity to begin to pursue your second-half mission. Go online to *www.halftime.org* and look under "Resources" for the capacity exercise.

5. Infusing fun into your life is an important element to finishing well. Identify three things you like to do to have fun. Approximately what percentage of your time is devoted to each one? Is that enough time, too little, or just right? What can you do to make it just right?

Chapter 17: Healthy Individualism

1. Bob says that the teaching that submission to Christ means "dying to self" is heresy and that in Christ's church, individualism is amplified, encouraged, supported, and complemented. Do you agree or disagree? In what ways is individualism a positive quality? In what ways can it be a problem?

2. How do you understand the difference between the smaller self and the larger self? In what ways is your first half focused on the smaller self? How can you sacrifice your small self for the larger self?

3. How will your second-half mission release your larger self?

4. Bob defines altruistic egoism as doing something for others both for their benefit and for your own. Can you think of examples where you did something difficult or challenging for the benefit of others yet benefited from it personally?

5. How can success lead to isolation and loneliness?

6. Think about the road signs that mark the difference between healthy and unhealthy individualism (see chart on page 141). Reading through this list, in which areas do you sense the need for improvement? What changes need to take place in your life to make those improvements?

Chapter 18: Lifelong Learning

1. Describe the relationship between what you learned in your undergraduate schooling and the current work you do.

2. What is the best form of learning that you have experienced since you began your career? Outside of your career, how much time do you spend learning new things for the sake of personal growth and enhancement?

3. As you consider your second-half mission, what new things will you have to learn to equip you for the challenges ahead? Make a list of at least three things and indicate how you think you will "train yourself" in those areas.

4. Review the list of ways to learn on pages 146–149. Which of these have been most helpful to you in the past? Which of these have you not really viewed or experienced as a way to learn? Why?

5. Does the prospect of having to learn new things for your second-half mission seem daunting, or does it create some excitement for you? Why?

Chapter 19: Respect for Externals

1. What have been the "externals" — the things in your current setting that cannot be changed?

2. Consider a situation in which you had a great idea but an "external" got in the way. For example, your boss said no, financing was unavailable, it would take you to an area far outside your expertise or comfort zone. How did you react to that barrier? What did you learn from the experience? How could you change the unchangeable externals in your life into opportunities?

3. Bob says that "there is no such thing as a life without authority." Do you agree? What authority or rules will you have to accept in your second-half mission?

4. The Bible teaches that the more you submit to the authority of Christ, the more radically free you become. How can that be true? Has this been true in your own life? Explain.

5. Describe the most unfair experience that has ever happened to you. How did you deal with the unfairness? What did you learn about yourself? About God? How are you discovering the grace and freedom to live with things that happen to you that seem unfair?

Chapter 20: Playing for All You're Worth

1. The noble idea of a life of significance soon translates into hard work and sacrifice. Thus you may be tempted to "dabble" in ministry so that it really doesn't cost you so much. It's like having one foot in the first half and one in the second. How are you avoiding the syndrome of keeping a foot in each half?

2. Bob warns that the transition from halftime into the second half may take a long time and include some false starts. Have you experienced that already? How does knowing this likelihood help you prepare to deal with it?

3. As you move into the second half, how might you be in all three places at once: first half, halftime, and second half?

4. The beauty of the second half is that it allows you to be your most authentic self. In what ways did the first half allow you to be authentic? In what ways did it prevent you from being authentic? How will your second half allow and encourage you to be your most authentic self?

5. Identify at least one quality about yourself that you are proud of but that sometimes was not allowed to really shine in your first half. How will you make sure this quality is allowed to drive your second half?

Chapter 21: The Money Question

1. Revisit your family budget to see what your actual needs are. Then consider adjusting your budget to allow for investing personal funds in your second-half mission.

2. Make a list of all the ways your career and financial situation might prevent you from entering halftime. Then go over that list and try to identify creative ways to overcome or minimize those barriers. Don't do it alone. Speak your confusion out loud to a trusted friend if only to hear your own reasoning.

3. Bob says that the potential rewards of halftime outweigh the risks involved. What rewards do you currently receive from your job? What rewards would you like to obtain from the skills and knowledge?

Chapter 22: A 50/50 Proposition

1. Do you truly believe "you have the freedom to decide whether you want the rest of your years to be the *best* of your years"? Identify three things that right now are either stopping you or causing you to hesitate to put your second-half game plan to work. For each of those barriers, identify one thing you will do over the next thirty days to overcome it.

2. How are your work, family, church, and community involvement integrated? How could they better integrate?

3. Describe at least one instance when you felt your faith was seen by someone in your community in a positive way. How did it make you feel?

4. Reread the last paragraph on page 167 where Bob recounts his vision for the Christian landscape. How can you capture this energy in your own life? What steps can you take to unleash it?

5. Bob writes that "individual responsibility is the key to transforming the church" (page 168). Consider your local church. What role and level of responsibility are you taking to change your church? The Halftime ministry provides detailed help for you as you consider a leadership role in your church or ministry. In particular, read our book *Unlimited Partnership*, available at *www.halftime.org*.

The Wisdom of Peter Drucker

by Bob Buford

As a young CEO in a rapidly changing cable television industry, I knew I needed a perspective wider than my own. The
year was 1984, and I had already become an ardent fan of the
writing of Peter Drucker, so I decided to take a chance and see if
he would be willing to consult with me. Thus began a wonderful relationship that continued until his death in 2005. As you
probably have already discovered from this book, his influence
on my life finds its way into nearly everything I have written,
and if you have ever heard me speak you know that I cannot get
very far into my comments without referencing this remarkable
man. Peter Drucker is the "intellectual father" of nearly all that
guides my philanthropy. In 1997, *Atlantic Monthly* editor Jack
Beatty interviewed me for two hours for a book he was writing,
The World According to Peter Drucker. That entire interview was
distilled into only six words from me that truly describe our relationship: "He's the brains, I'm the legs."

At the time of his death, at age ninety-five, Peter had taught
for more than thirty years at California's Claremont Graduate
School, where the Management Center is named after him. In addition to his career as a management professor — which includes
twenty years at New York University — he published more than
thirty books as well as articles for the *Wall Street Journal*, *Harvard Business Review*, *Forbes*, and many other periodicals — over
four million words altogether!

Peter approached his teaching, writing, and consulting as a journalist doing an in-depth story. He had an unparalleled grasp of the big picture and could tell you why the story was significant. He had the realism of a newsman but the ideals of a philosopher and the heart of a quietly committed Christian.

It would be difficult to capture in this brief space all that I have learned from Peter, but here are the highlights, especially as they relate to the halftime journey:

Mission Comes First

Largely due to his influence, "mission statements" are in vogue in most businesses today. But for Peter, a mission statement is more than ambitious intentions to be framed and hung on the board room wall. It is what drives everything the company does. Whether he was talking to CEOs, pastors, managers, or individuals contemplating a halftime experience, his counsel was always the same, "Don't ask 'what should I do,' but 'what needs doing?'" According to Peter, good intentions ("I want to do something significant") is only a starting point. The goal is results and performance that fulfills a clearly stated mission — something that needs doing — something that creates value for a customer. Peter told me over and over, "All results are on the outside. On the inside is only cost and effort."

Build on Islands of Health and Strength

When I began thinking about how I could focus my energy, talents, and resources on a more significant second half, I intuitively knew I wanted to work with churches. It was Peter who helped me see that I could accomplish more for God's Kingdom by working with larger, successful churches because these healthy institutions influence thousands of other churches. My mission was to release the latent energy in the church, and he showed me I could accomplish more and in less time by focusing on larger churches who had huge resources of latent energy just waiting to be released. "Work only on things that will make a great deal of difference if you succeed," he once told me. Similarly, Peter believed that individuals need to engage in second half careers built on the strengths and talents they already have. You do not have to reinvent yourself for a successful halftime; instead, you need to find ways to deploy your "best self" in new and significant ways.

Focus on Opportunities, Not Problems

According to Peter, most organizations assign their best resources to problems when, instead, they should direct their best people, thinking, and resources to find and exploit opportunities. Peter once told me, "Life is not that long. You can spend your whole life working with people who are receptive to what you want to do." He taught me not to spend priceless time being "against" or trying to convince people to do what they really didn't want to do. It was my work to find and connect energetic leaders who were receptive to the body of ideas called "Management" in order to build and multiply their growing, high energy churches. For the individual, Peter felt the most effective way to self renewal was to look for unexpected success and build on it. Peter taught me not to curse the darkness, but to run towards the light.

The "Parallel Career"

Peter was fascinated with the huge transition facing the Baby Boomers as they approached midlife. He accurately predicted that retirement would become increasingly unattractive to vibrant, healthy people who, as they approached their sixties, had reason to expect at least another twenty years of capacity and did not want to spend it in a rocking chair. It was Peter who helped me understand the concept of the "parallel career" — continuing with your present career as you explore new opportunities for the second half. Most people are unable to quit their "day job" and head into halftime, so the parallel career offers a realistic transition and eventually replaces the primary career.

The Shift from Industrial Work to Knowledge Work

Peter saw this coming well before we entered the "information age" and called it the most extreme societal change in recorded history. Previous generations really could not expect a vibrant and productive "second half" because their daily work simply wore them out. After twenty-five to thirty years working in a factory, tilling the fields, building highways, and so on, retirement was not only well earned but necessary. And brief, due to shorter life expectancy. Today, most workers sit at desks, attend meetings, negotiate the internet, and conduct business on cell phones — all using the same tool to grow their businesses: knowledge. By the time you hit your forties, you may be burnt out or sensing the need for a change, but physically you have yet to hit your peak and have at least another twenty-five years of high energy capacity before you. This one change is what led Peter to be so optimistic about the idea of halftime and predicted what has already begun happening: more and more successful people entering a second half of significance.

Planned Abandonment

Peter felt it was just as important — maybe more important — to decide what *not* to do as it was to decide *what* to do. Rick Warren, who also benefited from Peter's counsel, calls this "the power of no." The human tendency, largely driven by ego, is to believe we can do it all. When people approach me with a request to help them with a particularly exciting project, I have to recall Peter's advice to "get rid of investments in management ego" for projects that yield little results for the customer. It may be humbling to admit there are only a few things you do really well, but once you accept that fact, you will free yourself to focus on those things which will lead to greater personal success and significance.

The Role of the Social Sector

Most people think of Peter Drucker as the "father of modern management," which he was (though he was never very comfortable with that description). And while it's true that most of the very successful corporations owe a lot of their success to him, Peter increasingly turned his attention to the social sector — nonprofit organizations whose role is to look after the social needs of a culture. Peter felt strongly that while government has a critical role to play as policy maker, standard setter, and paymaster, it should not attempt to *run* social services because it has proven to be almost totally incompetent in that area. He also believed it was not a primary role of business to provide for the social needs of citizens. Instead, nonprofit agencies — of which more than fifty percent are churches and faith-based organizations — have the greatest potential for doing the greatest good. But as Peter would often say, "Don't mistake potential for performance," and devoted a great deal of his time helping the social sector, including churches, becoming more effective by becoming better managers. I know that some have criticized larger churches for becoming more "businesslike" by adopting modern management principles, but Peter was adamant that the function of management is to make the church more churchlike, not make it more businesslike. He saw such huge potential within churches to care for the social needs of the nation, especially within the ranks of Baby Boomers who will be looking for more meaningful options to retirement.

The Importance of the Customer

Peter was fond of three basic questions he would ask over and over: What is your business? Who is your customer? What does your customer value? To Peter, these three questions needed to be asked by the church as well. He believed an organization begins to die the day it begins to run for the benefit of the insiders and not for the benefit of the customers. Over the years, Leadership Network (www.leadnet.org), the organization I founded when I entered my second half, has gone through several strategic changes, many that were initiated by returning to those three questions.

Becoming an Adult

Peter once said to me, "The beginning of adult life is when you ask the question, 'What do I want to be remembered for?'" Essentially, this is the question of halftime. It speaks of legacy more than accomplishments and gets at the heart of significance. Nothing focuses your attention on legacy more than trying to write your own epitaph, which I shared with you in the Introduction to this book. It forces you, while in good health and decades ahead of you, to think about what matters most to you.

Peter was unconstrained by party, ideology, or prejudice. He was not, to use his own words, "a prisoner of his own predispositions." He taught me to recognize the need for continuous innovation; to always try to see things from different perspectives. He was, as he said in his book, *Adventures of a Bystander*, "Born to look. Meant to see." And because his vision was so clear, my life has been enriched beyond measure.

An Interview with Bob Buford

Zondervan: Bob, it's been almost fifteen years since you wrote *Halftime.* What's been going on in your own second half?

Buford: I wrote *Halftime* because I believe we live in an era when a person in his forties or fifties has at least three decades of high-capacity productivity ahead of them and that to simply look forward to retirement is not an acceptable option. So here I am in my third decade of my second half; I haven't retired. Instead I'm still working on things that provide immeasurable significance for me because they relate directly to my life mission, which is to release the latent energy in American Christianity. Specifically, that includes the work of Leadership Network, which provides resources and encouragement to pastors of large churches, and Halftime, Inc., which helps men and women successfully negotiate the journey from success to significance.

Zondervan: As you point out in *Halftime*, most people grow weary of their first-half lives. Now that you've been in your second half for thirty years, have you experienced any of the diminished interest that is so common in the first half.

Buford: Not at all, and the difference is the connection between the work I do and my passion, or mission. Significance. In the first half, the primary measure of my success was money and growth, and for a season those are powerful motivators, not only because it created wealth for me, but it provided jobs for my employees and value for our customers. I've never wanted to give the impression that there's anything wrong with striving for success in the first half, regardless of the work you do. It's just that at some point in the first half you begin to ask yourself, "Is this what I want to do for the rest of my life? Is this what I want to be remembered for?" It's what I call "success panic" — the realization that despite all your good work to provide for your family and contribute to your profession you may be missing out on things that are vastly more important. So even though I've been at this now for almost as long as I pursued my first-half career, I'm as engaged and energized as ever because the work I do is fully aligned with what matters to me most.

Zondervan: What about others? Are you seeing continued interest in the halftime concept?

Buford: Not only is there continued interest, but it is growing at a remarkable pace — to the point where I would call it a bona fide movement, one that will continue to grow since we are really only at the front end of the Boomer generation hitting middle age. As millions of men and women approach their fifth decade, they just know that there's a better way to live, and when they discover their second half of life can actually be better than their first half, the message of *Halftime* appeals to them.

I would also observe that the demographic window is widening. When I wrote Halftime, my focus was primarily on men in their early forties, but I'm seeing more women entering halftime as well as more and more men in their fifties and even sixties making the transition from success to significance.

Zondervan: Very few books remain in print for fifteen years, let alone continue to sell as well as *Halftime*. Are you surprised by this growing interest in *Halftime*, both the book and the movement?

Buford: Certainly I'm grateful, even humbled, by the book's success, but I'm not really surprised, because I learned to trust the instincts and knowledge of my good friend and mentor Peter Drucker. When I wrote *Halftime* in the early 1990s, Peter was about the only one who saw the future clearly enough to understand what was about to happen. At that time, my experience seemed unique, but Peter saw it as a template for the future.

Today you can hardly pick up a newspaper or magazine without seeing evidence that traditional retirement is just no longer an option. People want more out of life than a gold watch or a park bench. They want to be a part of something that contributes to others, which is why *Halftime* is so popular.

Zondervan: Aside from the sheer numbers of people approaching middle age, what other factors have contributed to this movement?

Buford: The shift away from traditional retirement to a second half of active, meaningful work comes from a convergence of three things that are happening in society; a "perfect storm" of factors that lead people into halftime: affluence, longevity, and "knowledge work." Even with the current economic uncertainties, people generally have enough wherewithal that they have options when they come to midlife. I think because of my own story, some people got the impression that you have to be wealthy to have the halftime experience, but we're seeing more and more people who can't quit their jobs and live off their wealth enjoying a dynamic second half doing work that fulfills their life mission. Ironically, a lot of people are being nudged into halftime by the very work they've been tied to. Typically, it happens this way: their company downsizes, they lose their job but are given a generous severance, but instead of trying to find another job they use their severance and imagination to develop a "parallel career." Similarly, many companies are offering early retirement with attractive buyouts to their senior-level employees, and very few of them jump back into another job somewhere. These are not wealthy people but they have enough affluence and opportunity to step back, reflect on what is most important to them, and then build a new career around that.

Zondervan: You mentioned longevity as a factor that is driving the halftime movement. By that, do you mean that people are living longer and thus have more time to pursue significance?

Buford: That's part of it, as clearly documented by today's Boomers living longer than their parents and grandparents. And it's actually pretty dramatic. Life expectancy in the early 1900s was fifty-six for men, and today it's seventy-six. So yes, we've been given at least an additional twenty years. But it's not just that we're living longer; we're living better. We're healthier and can expect to live active, dynamic lives well into our seventies and eighties. Just look at all the magazine and television ads aimed at people over sixty. They're playing tennis, climbing mountains, competing in marathons. If sixty is really "the new thirty," then think of the millions of people who even at retirement age will have twenty to thirty years of vitality and energy left in their tanks.

So for those who wait until "retirement" to experience half-time, the money question no longer becomes a barrier because they really *don't* have to work. This demographic could, in fact, become a new workforce of men and women in second-half careers that focus on their core values and altruistic instincts.

Zondervan: So this factor of longevity means if you're in your late fifties or sixties, you can still enter halftime?

Buford: Exactly. Timing is not as critical, especially for those who don't have a successful business to sell when they're forty and then go right into halftime. I mean, think about it. You're sixty-three, you're healthy, and between Social Security, whatever you've accumulated in your 401k, and most likely a significant inheritance, you really don't have to "work." And you have at least twenty good years ahead of you. Even if you buy the motor home and travel or take a couple of exotic cruises, most likely within a year you'll realize the "life of leisure" doesn't live up to its promise. If I could predict where the growth will be in people entering careers of significance, it would be in the sixty-plus category if only because of the sheer numbers of people currently entering that stage.

Zondervan: What do you mean by "knowledge work," and what role does that play in the increasing interest in halftime?

Buford: In previous generations, when manufacturing was king, most people worked with their hands. They worked in factories or built highways and skyscrapers or farmed the land. By the time they reached their fifties, they were worn out, so that retirement seemed attractive if for no other reason than they were tired and looked forward to a less physically demanding life. Today, we live in a cognitive world. People work in cubicles. They sit in front of computer screens, go to meetings, do their business over lunch. In fact, they have to look for ways to become physically active, thus the popularity of fitness centers and activities like jogging, bicycling, tennis, and hiking. People aren't worn out at fifty-eight, which is partly responsible for the longevity factor.

So, the prospect of leaving a first-half job to continue working in the second half is not daunting in the least and, in fact, is quite appealing. This cognitive age also opens up more opportunities for second-half work because knowledge workers are generally more adaptable, as long as they focus more on their strengths than their roles.

Zondervan: What do you mean by that?

Buford: Let's say you were a vice president of marketing in your first-half career. That's your role. If you view yourself solely in your role as a vice president of marketing, you will limit your opportunities for a meaningful second-half career because there probably are not too many organizations in the social sector looking for a vice president of marketing. But in that role, you most likely traded on your strengths of decision making, strategic planning, leadership, consumer needs, and communication. If you view yourself from the perspective of those strengths, you open up limitless possibilities for the second half because any one of those strengths will be valued by nonprofits. So while you might not end up as a vice president of marketing, you will have any number of opportunities to put those strengths to work in a calling that connects to what's most important to you.

A good example of that would be my friend, Steve Reineman, former CEO of Pepsico, who I interviewed in my book *Finish Well*. As he accepted invitations to speak on college campuses, he discovered a passion for working with young, energetic college students who, by the way, want their significance now. So when he left Pepsico he went into higher education, but not as the president, which would be playing to his role as a CEO. Instead, he's using his strengths to lead the Wake Forest University Business School as dean. That's not to say he couldn't have been a great college president, but he's fulfilling his passion of influencing students who will be tomorrow's business leaders, something he might not have been able to do as president.

Another way of thinking about strengths vs. roles is that whatever you have had for the last thirty years, you bring with you. Halftime helps you learn how to reformat those strengths to fit your second-half career.

Zondervan: It's probably fair to say you coined he phrase, "success to significance." In general, do you still believe people are interested in significance?

Buford: Yes, and I would point to two relatively new developments as proof. First, the way today's twenty-somethings want significance to the point they are not content to wait until midlife to pursue it. Nonprofit organizations like AmeriCorps and Teach for America report all-time high enrollments. Teach for America, which recruits teachers to fill difficult assignments in poverty-stricken rural and urban schools has to turn away 84 percent of its applicants because so many young teachers want to work in those environments. And nearly 250 colleges now offer courses in nonprofit management, with ninety offering graduate level courses as well. So clearly, significance is appealing to young people.

Second, we're seeing more and more people trying to work significance into their first-half careers. In a recent *Time* magazine cover story featuring the world's hundred most influential people, it struck me how their profiles focused on their contributions to other people rather than on their success. These were current CEOs, scientists, entrepreneurs, and entertainment personalities.

Zondervan: Now that you have the perspective of fifteen years to observe and coach people who have chosen the halftime experience, what have you learned?

Buford: The basic principles of moving from success to significance haven't changed. If anything, the desire for significance is even stronger and more universal than I once thought. Although I tried to prepare people for the challenges they will face in halftime, I realize now that it's not as easy as many people expect it will be. It takes time, a lot of careful and critical thinking, and often a few false starts.

Former Dallas Cowboys football player Bob Bruening — he was Roger Staubauch's roommate — went directly from his football career into the real-estate business, where he's been ever since. Contemplating a change, he told me, "I don't know what to do. For the past thirty one years I've been told what to do, when to practice, who and where to meet." Clearly an intelligent and capable guy, he had been totally programmed by his career. This is probably the biggest challenge going into halftime. We have to learn how to manage ourselves rather than let our work manage us. Halftime calls for introspection, listening to that still, small voice, more questions than answers — foreign territory in the first half.

Along these lines, I've learned that people tend to choose one of three options when they reach halftime. They either go away, go back, or go forward. Go away is what all the magazine advertisements recommend: "You'll have a pleasant second half if you move here." This is basically a retreat into "active leisure," and it has an almost magnetic appeal for many. Going back is what Peter Drucker called a "failure of the imagination." These are people who just can't imagine themselves making the adaptations necessary for a new season, so they go back to what they were doing before. Going forward offers both the excitement and fear that comes with any journey into uncharted territory, but it also promises the greatest rewards.

Zondervan: Do you think the current downturn in the economy will discourage people from trying the halftime experience?

Buford: No, because halftime isn't about money. Or to put it more positively, by the time a person enters his fourth or fifth decade, things like mission and meaning and passion become more important than successful careers or even wealth. I have a great story to illustrate this. John Snyder, who serves on the Leadership Network board, told me recently how in 2000 he sold his interest in an energy company when oil was $20 a barrel. If he had held onto that stock, and sold it in 2008 when oil hit $125 a barrel, he would have made a lot of money. As he put it, "If I'd stayed in the game, I'd be a billionaire today. But I'm glad I got out when I did because I would have missed the best years of my life." Instead of continuing with his highly stressful work, much of it away from home, he chose instead to spend as much time as he could with his wife, who died suddenly and unexpectedly one morning. He also formed a family foundation with his three sons and has now embarked on spending his next twenty-five years trying to start ten thousand free health-care clinics in churches to serve the poor and uninsured. "I couldn't have done any of that if I had stayed in the game," he told me.

John's story is an extreme example, but I see it happening at all levels. You reach a point where adding more zeroes to your net worth pales in comparison to significance.

Zondervan: In addition to your work with church leaders — your halftime mission — what are you doing to keep the halftime vision alive?

Buford: When I wrote *Halftime*, I immediately began hearing from people who either had questions or wanted to share their own experiences, so I sensed that *Halftime* had the potential to become more than just a book. I could spend the rest of my life talking to virtuous people who were making a difference in the lives of others, and thanks to the Internet, I found a way to do that through my website (*www.activeenergy.net*) which is technically an online newsletter, but I prefer to think of it as a confluence of explorers gathering occasionally around the fire to tell stories about what the natives are up to out there in this wonderful new life zone that I call "socially productive aging." Not only do I get to muse about whatever is on my mind, I get great feedback from those who post their responses.

I also started a new organization called the Halftime Group (formerly called FaithWorks) to help bring together high capacity leaders from the business/professional community with nonprofit leaders. With a very talented staff, I'm able to work more closely with individuals as they negotiate the transition from success to significance.

Finally, I continue to write. In 2004, I spent eighteen months interviewing 126 men and women who were at various stages of their second half careers, and that became the book *Finishing Well*. People like Ken Blanchard, Roger Staubach, Dallas Willard, and Jim Collins (who was kind enough to write a wonderful foreword to this edition of *Halftime*). Then in addition to the revision of this book, I wrote *Beyond Halftime* , which is my way of coming alongside people in halftime to offer encouragement, inspiration, and guidance.

Acknowledgments

In the process of working on this book and reviewing the facts of my life, I discovered a marvelous truth: I have never done anything important outside the context of a team. I think God must laugh at the seeming independence of us human beings who have such a tendency toward hubris and self-sufficiency. This may come from having made a lot of money, earning acclaim in sports, writing a book, or accomplishing something else extraordinary. God finds ways to teach all of us who are puffed up with ourselves how interdependent we really are.

Of all the writing on the interdependence of human beings, I think the greatest is by Paul in Romans 12, where he says:

> Do not think of yourself more highly than you ought, but rather think of yourself with sober judgment, in accordance with the faith God has distributed to each of you. For just as each of us has one body with many members, and these members do not all have the same function, so in Christ we, though many, form one body, and each member belongs to all the others. We have different gifts, according to the grace given to each of us. (vv. 3–6)

This book and the life it seeks to express are the product of a team. The credit for the book itself goes to Scott Bolinder, former publisher of Zondervan. I gave up on the book several times. He didn't, making a couple of visits to Dallas to talk the recalcitrant "author" into getting the book done. Lyn Cryderman did the crafting. My assistant, B. J. Engle, has spent hours drafting and redrafting the multiple manuscripts. I learned firsthand what T. S. Eliot meant when he called writing a "raid on the inarticulate."

I am part of several teams for different purposes. For life planning, Peter Drucker has been the most important person in my life. Early on, when I needed desperately to learn how to manage a business, he was my teacher, as he has been for so many through his books. Later in life, as I entered my second half, Peter became my guide in the shift from success to significance. Of the many books in my office, two have become my greatest companions: Peter Drucker's large book *Management* as my guide for human things and the Bible as my guide for spiritual things. Peter died to this life in November 2005, just short of his ninety-fifth birthday. His ideas live on in his written legacy and in the lives he touched.

It is enough to have written the book just to carry Peter Drucker's foreword into your hands. It says so much that is priceless to me but, more important, so much that is valuable to you. It allows Peter to be your guide in interpreting what is happening, as he has been mine for years.

This new edition of *Halftime* is begun with a new foreword by Jim Collins, the current star in the management field. Like Peter's, Jim's eyes see more than those of most anyone else. My first team, of course, is that with my wife, Linda. She is a completely distinct individual, very much unlike me (thank God), but there are times when I can't tell where my thoughts stop and hers begin. I couldn't begin to imagine life without this person whom I love and respect so much. And, of course, Ross, my son, whom I lost physically in 1987, is still very much with me. In many ways Ross was the uncompleted part of my personality — physical, springing with vitality, passionate, a lover of men, women, and hunting dogs. It won't be long in the whole scheme of things until I see him again. We will share eternity together.

And most of all, I want to presume to acknowledge the partnership of God. It is inexpressible joy and unspeakable pleasure to feel that I — little finite me — am in partnership with the very Creator of the universe. I didn't quite realize this relationship until I read Peter Drucker's foreword for this book. He speaks of a book that is much more than a book that I am capable of writing. I tried, and I couldn't do it. I found it too much for my skills, yet here it is. And for that amazing fact, I can only be grateful to God. Good job, God.

Notes

Part 1, The First Half

Chapter 1, *Listening to the Gentle Whisper*

1. Connie Goldman, *The Ageless Spirit* (Minneapolis: Fairview, 2004).

Chapter 6, *"Adios, Ross"*

1. John Donne, *Meditation XVII*.

Part 2, Halftime

Chapter 7, *Taking Stock*

1. From a brochure no longer available.

Chapter 9, *Finding Your One Thing*

1. *City Slickers*, directed by Ron Underwood, screenplay by Lowell Ganz and Babaloo Mandel (Hollywood: Columbia Pictures, 1991).
2. Eric Hoffer, *Reflections on the Human Condition* (New York: Harper-Collins, 1973).
3. Larry Crabb, *Inside Out* (Colorado Springs: NavPress, 1984).

Chapter 10, *From Success to Significance*

1. Dennis O'Connor and Donald M. Wolf, "From Crisis to Growth at Midlife: Changes in Personal Paradigm," *Journal of Organizational Behavior* 12, no. 4 (July 1991): 323–40.

Chapter 11, *Finding the Center and Staying There*

1. Laura Nash, *Believers in Business* (Nashville: Nelson, 1994).

Chapter 13, *Overlapping Curves*

1. Charles Handy, *The Age of Paradox* (Watertown, Mass.: Harvard Business School Press, 1995).

Chapter 14, Leaping into the Abyss

1. Dag Hammarskjold, *Markings* (New York: Knopf, 1964).

Part 3, The Second Half

Chapter 15, Life Mission

1. Steven R. Covey, *The Seven Habits of Highly Effective People* (New York: Simon and Schuster, 1986).
2. Andrew Carnegie, *Round the World* (Charleston, S.C.: Biblio Bazaar, 2007).
3. Richard Nelson Bolles, *What Color Is Your Parachute?* (Berkeley: Ten Speed, 2007).

Chapter 16, Regaining Control

1. Charles Handy, *The Age of Unreason* (Watertown, Mass.: Harvard Business School Press, 1990).
2. Mihaly Csíkszentmihályi, *The Evolving Self* (New York: HarperCollins, 1993).
3. Robert Bellah and others, *Habits of the Heart* (New York: HarperCollins, 1988).

Chapter 17, Healthy Individualism

1. Hans Selye, *The Stress of Life* (New York: McGraw-Hill, 1978).

Chapter 18, Lifelong Learning

1. Peter Senge, *The Fifth Discipline* (New York: Doubleday, 1990).

Selected Bibliography

Blanchard, Ken. *Lead Like Jesus.* Nashville: Nelson, 2007. (Including the *Lead Like Jesus* study guide.)

Bolles, Richard Nelson. *What Color Is Your Parachute? A Practical Manual for Job-Hunters and Career Changers.* Berkeley: Ten Speed, 2007.

Brafman, Ori, and Rod A. Beckstrom. *Starfish and the Spider: The Unstoppable Power of Leaderless Organizations.* New York: Penguin, 2006.

Brooks, David. *On Paradise Drive.* Farmington Hills, Mich.: Gale, 2004.

Buckingham, Marcus, and Donald O. Clifton. *Now Discover Your Strengths.* New York: Simon and Schuster, 2001.

Collins, Jim. *Good to Great for the Social Sector.* New York: Harper-Collins, 2005.

Drucker, Peter. *The Effective Executive.* New York: HarperCollins, 2006.

Drucker, Peter with Joseph A. Maciariello, *Management, Revised Edition.* Watertown, Mass.: HarperBusiness, 2008.

Edersheim, Elizabeth. *The Definitive Drucker.* New York: McGraw-Hill, 2006.

Ellis, Charles, and John J. Brennan. *Winning in a Loser's Game.* New York: McGraw-Hill, 2002.

Fournier, Ron, Douglas B. Sosnik, and Matthew J. Dowd. *Applebee's America.* New York: Simon and Schuster, 2007.

Handy, Charles. *The Age of Paradox.* Watertown, Mass.: Harvard Business School Press, 1995.

——. *The Age of Unreason.* Watertown, Mass.: Harvard Business School Press, 1990.

Johansson, Frans. *The Medici Effect.* Watertown, Mass.: Harvard Business School Press, 2006.

Kim, Chan W., and Renee Mauborgne. *Blue Ocean Strategy.* Watertown, Mass.: Harvard Business School Press, 2005.

Maciariello, Joseph A., ed. *The Daily Drucker.* New York: Harper-Collins, 2004.

McNeal, Reggie. *Present Future Church.* Hoboken, N.J.: John Wiley & Sons, 2003.

Reeb, Lloyd. *From Success to Significance.* Grand Rapids, Mich.: Zondervan, 2004.

Rilke, Rainer Maria. Ulrich Baer, ed. and trans. *The Poet's Guide to Life: The Wisdom of Rilke.* New York: Random House, 2005.

Thumma, Scott, Travis Davis, and Rick Warren. *Beyond Megachurch Myths.* San Francisco: Jossey-Bass, 2007.

Warren, Rick. *The Purpose-Driven Life.* Grand Rapids, Mich.: Zondervan, 2002.

Epilogue

*The 20th century is the first in which substantial
and rapidly growing numbers of people have real choices
about how they will invest their time and talent....
Most people are totally unprepared for it.*
—Peter Drucker, *Managing Oneself*

Dear Reader:

Thank you for reading *Halftime*. If you take the message of this book seriously, you are about to embark on one of the most exciting and rewarding journeys of your life. It won't always be easy, but it will be fulfilling. Stay faithful.

My life is an example of the fact that halftime is an ongoing journey. In July 1999 I sold my company, which means I am officially in halftime on a full-time basis. I am personally still learning how to navigate, and I am learning from other people as they share their halftime struggles and victories with me. We need to learn from and support one another, so I began to develop organizations and tools that would help you and others like you to respond to the opportunities presented on your halftime journey.

Each organization or tool is designed to give you guidelines, ideas, and real-life experiences to help you get started and stay committed along the way. I hope they are helpful to you.

I wrote **Game Plan** in 1997 to give people more specific "how-to" guidance through questions, recommended actions, and fill-in-the-blank self-directed exercises, which people had asked me to provide.

Halftime.org is one of the tools developed in response to the demand created by *Halftime*. After reading the book, many people asked for assistance with three key areas:

1. assessing giftedness
2. developing a vision of what the second half could be
3. knowing how to make a solid "next step" for beginning the process

As a result, *Halftime.org* is a Web-based interactive coach to help people navigate the challenges that halftime presents.

Halftime (*www.Halftime.org*) is a unique organization that was founded to inspire business and professional leaders to embrace God's calling and move from success to significance. This is accomplished through events, networking, and transitional strategies to connect business and professional leaders with God's unique calling for their lives.

If you experience a Halftime event, chances are it will completely redefine for you what an exhilarating and eternally significant second half can look like. The inspirational stories of what others have done at halftime combined with a comprehensive assessment of your gifts and passions can lead to a second-half mission statement that will get you focused on what God is calling you to do. And high-touch follow-up will enable you to gain the insights of fellow business and professional leaders for your halftime transition.

Ultimately, Halftime will help you connect with others who desire to put their faith into action. Events are offered locally around the country.

Stuck in Halftime: Reinvesting Your One and Only Life. Since writing *Halftime*, I have had countless interviews with people who immediately identified with the concept of halftime.

They started the journey but then became stuck. I have been able to help some of them get "unstuck." This book identifies some of the false paths and myths that lead people away from a second half of significance. It will give you some ideas on how to turn your second-half dream into reality. It will also give you real-life examples of people who have successfully navigated halftime.

Many people have expressed an interest in other endeavors in which I am involved. The following initiatives reflect my interests both as an entrepreneur and as someone wanting to make a difference through the application of my faith and resources under the general mission of transforming the latent energy of the American church into active energy. For more information on a specific initiative, visit the website address provided. I also would encourage you to directly contact the organization.

Leadership Network (*www.leadnet.org*). Started in 1984, Leadership Network serves as a resource broker that supplies information to and connects leaders of innovative churches. The emerging new paradigm of the twenty-first-century church calls for the development of new tools and resources as well as the equipping of a new breed of twenty-first-century church leader, both clergy and laity. Leadership Network serves the leadership teams of large churches, as well as leaders in the areas of lay mobilization, denominational leadership at the middle and regional judicatory level, and the next generation of emerging young leaders.

Leader to Leader, formerly the Peter F. Drucker Foundation for Nonprofit Management (*www.pfdf.org*). In 1988 Dick Schubert, Frances Hesselbein, and I convinced Peter Drucker to lend his name, his great mind, and occasionally his presence to establish an operating foundation for the purpose of leading social sector organizations toward excellence in performance. I serve as the founding chairman of the board of governors. Through its conferences, publications, and partnerships, Leader to Leader is helping social sector organizations focus on their mission, achieve true accountability, leverage innovation, and develop productive partnerships.

ACTIVEenergy (*www.activeenergy.net*). This is my own webpage with links to many other sites that will help you on your halftime journey. I am writing "my next book" in real time on this website with new chapters that will come to you by email. It is free, and all the prior chapters are archived here. Although I will continue writing my "musings" here, my next book is actually based on these musings and will be released soon as *Beyond Halftime*.

The Drucker Institute (*www.druckerinstitute.com*). In May of 2006 the Drucker Archive reconstituted as the Drucker Institute, upon which I now serve as the Chairman of the Board. The Institute was charged with taking Peter's teachings and ideals to "new audience in new ways." Today the Institute has various programs and channels including a network of Drucker Societies all around the globe. In addition to the think-tank and action-tank activities of the Institute, it houses the priceless online archive of Peter's work.

• • •

On a personal note, as you start your journey from success to significance, begin with the end in mind. The end I see for me is that in due course I'm going to be rejoined with Ross and other friends and family with the heavenly host. That's not a day I dread; I'll be happy. Think of me as being happy. Think of me as being accountable, as *wanting* to be accountable. I think there is going to be a final exam just before entry into the next level — with just two questions.

The first question is, "What did you do about Jesus?" Did you accept him, or did you just blow him off and say you were too busy or unavailable?

The second question is, "What did you do with what I gave *you* to work with?" Not your friends, not your work associates, not your family — *you!*

That's my word of wisdom for you — think ahead to that moment in your life and take steps now to be well prepared for the final exam so that you will hear the words "Well done, good and faithful servant."

BOB BUFORD
November 2008

The Halftime organization has people all over the world to assist your transition from Success to Significance®.

See where Halftime branches are located:
www.halftime.org/locations

If you are interested in establishing a Halftime branch near you, contact us:
www.halftime.org/contact-us

More resources for your Halftime journey:

Executive Coaching: professionally trained and certified Halftime Coaches can help you have a second half of impact:
www.halftime.org/coaching

Executive Search: Halftime Talent Solutions places professionals in fulfilling leadership positions with non-profits:
www.halftimetalent.com

You've read the book... What's next?

Bob Buford hosts the Halftime Institute
several times a year in Dallas, Texas USA.

The Halftime Institute is a powerful, two-day deep dive
into how you are wired with skills, passions, and a calling.
Those who attend the Institute with Bob and a small
group of peers get accelerated traction toward
understanding God's purpose for their second half.

For upcoming dates and to register:
www.halftime.org/the-halftime-institute

Many people ask Bob,
"When are you going to write your next book?"
He is doing it on the Web, a chapter at a time:
www.ACTIVEenergy.net